From Childhood to *Adolescence*

Including Erdkinder and
The Function of the University

MARIA MONTESSORI

SCHOCKEN BOOKS • NEW YORK

First English edition 1973

Library of Congress Catalog Card No. 72–91607

Translated from the French by
The Montessori Educational Research Center

Manufactured in the United States of America

WE ARE VERY happy that this book, *From Childhood to Adolescence,* is being published by Schocken Books Inc. The Association Montessori Internationale is now actively joining with Schocken Books to promote the works of Maria Montessori in the English language. We hope that this book will be followed by others illustrating various aspects of the Montessori approach to education as a help to life.

MARIO M. MONTESSORI,
General Director
Association Montessori Internationale

Contents

Publisher's Note

IN *From Childhood to Adolescence,* Maria Montessori applies her genius to the educational concerns of the older child—the adolescent and even the mature university student. At each level she looks at matters not from the point of view of the teacher seeking ways and means of transmitting the cultural heritage to the next generation, but rather from that of a clear-eyed scientist concerned with the unfolding and growth of that complex organism we call man. For each stage she seeks ways to facilitate optimum development.

As early as 1920, only thirteen years after the first *casa dei bambini* opened its doors to very young slum children in Rome, Montessori turned her attention to education at the highest level. At that time she reached an agreement with the University of Amsterdam to develop her work on university lines; it was also in Holland that the government endorsed Montessori methods at all educational levels and that a system of Montessori schools from preschool through lyceum (high school) came into existence.

Broadly grouping developmental levels, as does Piaget, Montessori first discusses the characteristics and needs of children from seven to twelve, showing that when a special environment is provided, the preadolescent is able and eager to apply himself to fields of study that have usually been reserved for the high school years. She finds that his interest in the world about him naturally leads him to inquire into the earth sciences and into experimentation and study in such areas as organic and inorganic chemistry. As examples, she presents several chapters dealing with subject matter that might be appropriate at this level. Her approach is similar to that of Jerome Bruner's spiral curriculum. On presenting a new concept, she says: "This idea remains indefinite in the imagination of the child but it corresponds to reality. Given that each of the details is later studied, it causes him to remember this view of the whole. So the knowledge, carrying its conclusions, radiates as though from a center, much as a seed develops little by little."

Montessori's ideas for the education of adolescents are as startlingly new today as her *casa dei bambini* was in 1907. The specific proposals, here included in the Appendix, were first published in Amsterdam in 1939 under the titles "The Erdkinder: A Scheme for a Reform of Secondary Education," "The Reform of Education During and After Adolescence," and "The Function of the University." In them she puts forth an "experimental school of social life," a school utterly different from our secondary schools. Her criticism of accepted practice is devastating: "The secondary school, such as it is at present, has no other aim than to prepare the pupils for a career, as if the social conditions of our lives were still peaceful and stable. . . . Not only does it not correspond to the social conditions of our day, but it is utterly bankrupt before the task it will have to take on: to protect and encourage the blossoming of the personalities of adolescents, the human energy on which the future depends." Today, decades later, it is only in the one area of health that we have solved problems that concerned Montessori. No longer do we see adolescence as a period when health is precarious, no longer does the specter of tuberculosis loom before us.

Montessori sees adolescence as the "sensitive period" for

social relationships, the age at which the child must make a place for himself with his peers and at which he begins to consider the social realities of the wider community. Her experimental school for social life would be in a rural setting, where children and their predominantly young teachers would live in a self-contained community, self-governing and to a considerable extent self-supporting. Raising their own foodstuffs and perhaps running a guest house or store, they would learn about the work of the world at first hand.

Preparation for university entrance examinations would be provided for those students who wished to continue their education; it would coincide with the end of adolescence, when motivation for academic subjects is at its highest, much as it does at A. S. Neill's Summerhill School. Montessori believed that many universities of her day were merely diploma-granting institutions providing little more than an entry ticket into the professions and ignoring their true function: to prepare young adults, who are treated as adults, for a lifetime of research and inquiry.

Like much of Dr. Montessori's published work, this book bears the earmarks of her dynamic personality. She was an extraordinarily gifted and dramatic lecturer, and, although she knew several languages, she lectured in Italian and had a translator share the platform. It was often the transcriptions of these lectures, with little or no editing, that were turned into books.

The present book shows evidence that it was conceived as a series of lectures. These were assembled and translated into French, and first published in 1948. This English edition, translated from the French, makes *From Childhood to Adolescence* available to the English-speaking world for the first time. In it, Maria Montessori clearly speaks to the problems of our time, giving us new insights into what some of the unrest and dissatisfaction in our schools and colleges is all about.

MY VISION OF THE FUTURE is no longer of people taking exams and proceeding on that certification from the secondary school to the university, but of individuals passing from one stage of independence to a higher, by means of their own activity, through their own effort of will, which constitutes the inner evolution of the individual.

—MARIA MONTESSORI

From Childhood
to Adolescence

1

The Successive Levels
of Education

The Successive Levels
of Education

THE SUCCESSIVE levels of education must correspond to the successive personalities of the child.

Our methods are oriented not to any principles but rather to the inherent characteristics of the different ages. It follows that these characteristics themselves include several levels.

The different ages could be compared to the metamorphoses of insects. When an insect comes out of the egg, it is very small and has a particular form and coloring. Then, little by little, it is transformed even though it remains an animal of the same species having the same needs and habits. It is an individual that *evolves.* Then one day something new happens. The insect spins his cocoon and becomes a chrysalis. The chrysalis in turn undergoes another slow evolution. Finally the insect comes out of the cocoon in the form of a butterfly.

We can establish a parallel between the life of the insect and that of the child. But the changing traits are not so clearly defined in the child as in the insect. It would be more exact to speak rather of the "rebirth" of the child. In effect, we have before us at each new stage a different child who presents characteristics different from those he exhibited during preceding years.

1. Our first level of education, then, applies to the small

child from birth to about seven years of age. Since a number of transformations take place during this important period, we have established the following subdivisions:

a) the first two years;
b) the years from three to five;
c) the sixth and seventh years.

2. The period from seven to twelve years—the period immediately preceding adolescence—may also be subdivided. It is on a different level than the preceding period. If the changes produced during the first period are considered as growth, it may be said that veritable metamorphoses take place during this one.

3. Twelve to eighteen years: one could say as much for this, the period of adolescence.

In each period we rediscover a growing being, but one who is a quite different person every time.

The last two levels will be considered consecutively. The first level has already been discussed in *The Discovery of the Child*.

Only a thorough analysis leads to the discovery of the changes that occur continuously in the child, who grows until he becomes a man. It is precisely these changes that have the greatest bearing on the method of education.

The principles that can be applied usefully to the first period are not the same as those that must be applied to the second. We thus come to the practical part of education.

Let us use an example: When the small child begins to feel a loose tooth, it is a sign that the first period of childhood is over. This event occurs without much fanfare within the family. When the tooth becomes very loose it is pulled. A certain amount of fuss is made: the tooth is saved, and that little ceremony constitutes the first step of a new period in the life of the child. It will take a long time before all the baby teeth are gone and the child acquires his new teeth. But if, unluckily, it is necessary to pull one of the new teeth, more will be needed than merely a silk thread; we will have to deal with the extraction of a strong and fixed part. Loss of the baby teeth is only one among the many manifestations of this age. All these traits —physical as much as psychic—constitute the links of the chain which is the metamorphosis of the child. He is both stronger and slimmer. His hair is less lovely. Psychologically, he is less gentle, less agreeable.

2

Metamorphoses

Metamorphoses

FROM SEVEN to twelve years, the child needs to enlarge his field of action. As we have seen (in *The Secret of Childhood*), the closed environment is suited to the small child. There, social relations are established with others. In the second period the child needs wider boundaries for his social experiences. Development cannot result by leaving him in his former environment.

It is necessary that he come to understand, among other realities, what money ought to represent. Without money we could pass among the most marvelous things without ever being able to touch them. We would be like a bird with a broken wing dying of hunger on a pile of grain. Money is the means by which man procures things. That is why it attracts so much interest. We must consider money as the "key metal" that opens the door.

It is therefore necessary that children have first-hand experience in buying objects themselves and that they come to realize what they can buy with a unit of the money of their country.

What can one buy with one small coin? When I have used the coin to buy paper from the stationer, my coin has not disappeared. It will again buy more objects of its value. It is always the same coin that passes from hand to hand, bringing a needed article to someone every time. How much merchandise could a coin of the same denomination have bought fifty years ago? The money we handle is always the result of the work of men. It must always remain a means.

The child needs, then, to establish social relationships in a larger society. The closed school, as it is conceived today, can no longer be sufficient for him. Something is lacking for the full development of his personality. We note a certain regression—manifestations of his character which we call anomalies; they are merely his reactions to an environment that has become inadequate. But we do not notice that. And since it is understood that the child must do what adults tell him, even though his environment no longer suits his needs, if he does not comply we say that he is "naughty" and correct him. Most of the time we are unaware of the cause of his "naughtiness." Yet the child, by his conduct, proves what we have just said. The closed environment is felt as a constraint, and that is why he no longer wishes to go to school. He prefers to catch frogs or play in the street. These seemingly superficial factors prove that the child needs wider boundaries than heretofore.

"Render unto Caesar the things that are Caesar's, and to God the things that are God's." One part of our life belongs to God and the other part to man. It depends on him, on the surroundings of which we form a part, on our social life. When the child is placed in certain conditions that favor him, he manifests an extraordinary activity. His intelligence surprises us because all its functions work in pairs, as is normal for man. We are no longer dealing with the problem of transforming the methods of education: it is properly a problem of life that is being posed.

The spider's web occupies a much larger space than does the animal itself. The web represents the spider's field of action in acting as a trap for insects. It is constructed according to a plan. A thread secreted by the spider joins two branches, two rocks, two supports of any kind; then he weaves the rays. The construction proceeds according to a plan. Finally the spider weaves the thread around the center, going around at an always very carefully calculated distance. If the points of support are close together, the web is small. The greater the distance of one from the other, the larger the web will be. But it will always be woven with the same exactness according to the same plan.

As is the web, so is the mind of the child constructed according to an exact plan. The abstract construction enables him to grasp what happens in his field, which was out of his range heretofore.

Depending on whether the child lives in a simple civilization or in a complicated world, his web will be more or less large and will enable him to attain more or fewer objectives.

This is why we must respect the interior construction and its manifestations, which may at times seem useless to us. The construction is necessary. It is thanks to this work that the child enlarges his psychic field and subsequently his receptive powers.

To consider the school as the place where instruction is given is one point of view. But to consider the school as a preparation for life is another. In the latter case the school must satisfy all the needs of life.

An education that suppresses the true nature of the child is an education that leads to the development of anomalies.

Scouting, which, outside of school, has brought organized activity to children, has always interested us.

The passage to the second level of education is the passage from the sensorial, material level to the abstract. The need for abstraction and intellectual activity makes itself felt around the seventh year, which is just the age when the establishment of the relationships between objects is what is important to the child. This is to say that the child needs to classify and absorb the exterior world by means of his senses.

A turning toward the intellectual and moral sides of life occurs at this age.

One could draw a parallel between the two periods. But they still remain on different levels. It is at seven years that one may note the beginning of an orientation toward moral questions, toward the judgment of acts. One of the most curious characteristics to be observed is the interest that occurs in the child when he begins to perceive things which he previously failed to notice. Thus he begins to worry about whether what he has done has been done well or poorly. The great problem of Good and Evil now confronts him. This preoccupation belongs to an interior sensitivity, the conscience. And this sensitivity is a very natural characteristic.

The seven-to-twelve-year-old period, then, constitutes one of particular importance for moral education. The adult must be aware of the evolution that is occurring in the mind of the child at this time and adapt his methods to conform with it.

If during the first period of development the teacher has used very gentle methods and has intervened as little as possible in the activity (activity which was motor and sensorial), it is to the moral level that his very gentle methods ought now to be oriented. That is where the problem of this age lies. To think that the problem of morality only occurs later is to overlook the change that is already going on. Later, the moral problem becomes a good deal more difficult unless the child has been helped during the sensitive period. Social adaptations will become more thorny. It is at this age also that the concept of justice is born, simultaneously with the understanding of the relationship between one's acts and the needs of others. The sense of justice, so often missing in man, is found during the development of the young child. It is the failure to recognize this fact that engenders a false idea of justice.

The justice usually found around the school and in the family could be called "distributive justice"—that is to say, equality for all, as much in the distribution of punishments as of rewards. Special treatment of one individual seems to constitute an injustice; this introduces the concept of right. There is here an affirmation of individuality in the sense of egoism and isolation. Such a concept does not encourage interior development. On the other hand, justice—although usually not considered in this light—is born specifically from interior education. The principle of distributive justice and individual right, purely external, destroys the inborn, natural sense of true justice.

3

The Moral Characteristics of the Child from Seven to Twelve Years

The Moral Characteristics
of the Child from
Seven to Twelve Years

THE THREE characteristics we have just isolated for examination
—the child's felt need to escape the closed environment, the
passage of his mind to the abstract, and the birth in him of a
moral sense—serve as the basis for a scheme of the second
period.

Once the child is outside the limited area of the first period,
it is necessary for us to provide him with culture and to enlarge
his social experiences. Let us cite some important points and
note, in passing, the parallel that exists between this new period
and certain aspects of the preceding one.

Actually, the first period saw the child in activities which we
have called "experiences of practical life." They constituted an
effort to stretch the limits of the activities we considered possible
for him at that age. In this way the child, who has himself
stretched the limits, has won his independence. This is what
makes these exercises of patience, of exactness, and of repetition
so all-important.

The continuation of these exercises would be useless now
that the child is independent; that is to say, he knows how to
devote himself to an activity for which he will not need to ask
help of the adult and for which he has coordination of movement. But the acts of courtesy which he has been taught with

a view to his making contacts with others must now be brought to a new level. The question of aid to the weak, to the aged, to the sick, for example, now arises. This is not a question of exercising his movements: we begin the introduction of moral relationships, of those that awaken the conscience. If, up to the present, it was important not to bump someone in passing, it is now considerably more important not to offend that person.

If scouting has met with such success, it is because it has brought moral content to a group of children. It puts the accent on that which one ought or ought not to do. The children who belong to these groups generally do not do what scouting prohibits. In conforming to the rules of scouting, a new dignity is born in the child.

Physical exercise, such as long hikes, also forms a part of the activities of these groups. The children become hardened and accustomed to greater challenges.

While the younger child seeks comforts, the older child is now eager to encounter challenges. But these challenges must have an aim. The difference between a schoolteacher who takes children on a hike and an organization of this nature may be noted here. It is true that the former makes the children come out of the closed environment of the school and causes them to use their feet in walking and to see sensorially that which surrounds them. But this in no way increases the dignity of the child, who is still kept in a restricted circle. One may well multiply the number of hikes without changing anything, because the child's presence is passive. On the other hand, if the children consciously leave the school having a definite and freely chosen aim in mind, it is quite a different matter.

Now, scouting involves children who have joined voluntarily in the society. And that society emphasizes, above all, a moral aim such as, for example, to protect the weak and to maintain a certain moral level; here the child may make commitments or not. No teacher obliges him to enter into the society; but it is his own scoutmaster whom he must obey in these principles if he wishes to take part. The fact that he finds himself thus united with other individuals who have freely accepted the principles of a society constitutes the attraction of that society. Its limits are no longer the walls of a room but only the restraints of moral order.

The scouts accept a regimen the rigors of which are surprising for children of this age. Thus the long hikes, the nights in the open air, the responsibility for one's own actions, the fire, the camps, et cetera, all represent collective efforts. The basic moral principle requires a commitment from the individual: the commitment of the individual to the group. And that is what is essential.

As in the first period: We seek the child's consent to receive a lesson given. The lesson is now abstract when earlier it was sensorial.

In the second period there exist, then, possibilities superior to those we used to know in the child. Only, these possibilities are subordinate not to the command of someone, but rather to the command of the child's own conscience.

4

*The Needs of the Child
from Seven to Twelve Years*

The Needs of the Child
from Seven to Twelve Years

WHAT IS the practical approach to the education of a seven-year-old? First of all, let us always keep in mind the scheme we have just outlined, which ought to give us an understanding of the child and to let us help him in the attainment of his wishes—wishes he does not express but which we have guessed. It is this understanding that ought to be present in the beginning. We must sympathize with the little boy or girl who has changed, as much in his physical aspect (manner of dress, of combing his hair, et cetera) as in his inner person. He has become a strong being, a being who is entering into a new world, the world of the abstract. It is a rich world in which the acts accomplished by men will interest him more than the things. He is growing and he will think independently. This is new for him. Before, he was interested in things (changing the water for flowers, caring for the little fish, et cetera). Now he will occupy himself mainly with the how and the why. All that used to attract him sensorially now interests him from a different point of view. He is looking for what needs to be done. That is, he is beginning to become aware of the problem of cause and effect.

But the adult finds this being, newly born to the world, a bit annoying. Therefore, without a new pedagogic directive, a new battle between the adult and this new child arises. The adult tires and responds by answering the abundance of questions either by begging the child to keep quiet or by giving excessively long explanations. He behaves as he did with the smaller child at the time he began to move: he bids him to keep still. Or he permits him, without judging properly, to become overexcited and to do everything he wants. The same misunderstanding takes place on the abstract plane: at each of his new births the child must confront a new battle; at each of his new activities, however valuable, a new problem arises for him. It is up to the adult to assist the child's development by creating an environment adapted to his new needs. Just as it is necessary to help the baby while he is taking his first steps, so is it also necessary to help the child while he is taking his first steps in the world of abstraction.

Education ought to be a guide in this more critical period of life and of school. The teacher must also be made aware of his limitations, as we have already established with regard to the teacher of the smaller child. For the small child, he had to "count his words." Here he must be sure of what he ought to do, of what he ought to say, and of the extent to which he must reply to questions. He must be clearly conscious that his duty is to say little; to say only what is "necessary and sufficient." It is indispensable to the child to feel the self-confidence of the adult.

It is essential for the child, in all periods of his life, to have the possibility of suitable activities in order to preserve the equilibrium between acting and thinking. His thoughts could, in effect, have the tendency to lose themselves in abstraction by reasonings without end just as the small child loses himself in a world of fantasy. We bring specific objects to the small child in an environment prepared for him. Here he acquires independence thanks to his own effort. And the activity gives him dignity. It is his own experience that brings him exact answers.

The role of education is to interest the child profoundly in an external activity to which he will give all his potential. We are concerned here with bringing him liberty and independence while interesting him in an activity through which he will subsequently discover reality. And for him this is the means by which he may free himself from the adult.

Let us examine the principal needs of the seven-year-old child. Something has changed in the body of this child. We see the difference at first glance in the teeth and the hair. Let us teach him dental hygiene and care of the hair. Then the feet and legs: the child of seven years has strong legs and seeks to escape from the closed circle. Instead of hemming him in, let us facilitate his mobility. In times gone by, man used to walk long distances. The hospitality offered the pilgrim used to consist first of all in the care of the feet, even before the offer of food. Let us give our imaginations free rein on the subject of these fundamentals of the history of humanity. Gabriel d'Annunzio used these symbolic words: "I kiss your feet that walk . . ."

Therefore, when the child shows us his desire to escape from the house, let us attract his attention somewhat solemnly to his feet. Thus, before setting out, he will be more conscious of what he is about to do. In attracting his attention to this part of his body, which may cause him to make a mistake, we lead him to think of the need to care for it, in order to walk, as much symbolically as practically.* It is on a higher plane that all these activities ought to be envisaged, which is to say, we will now educate the child on the abstract plane.

The foot is noble. To walk is noble. Thanks to the feet, the child who already walks can expect of the outdoors certain answers to his secret questions.

But it is necessary to prepare oneself to go out. The child

* Similarly, many modern schools teach rules of bicycle safety and maintenance.—TR.

in flight opens the door and goes. In teaching him the necessity of preparation, we oblige him to reflect. He understands that "to go out" consists of an activity that requires first the acquisition of information and materials.

The use of these things causes a series of practical exercises to come to mind. While for the very young the care of the wardrobe remains purely esthetic, for the seven-year-old, clothes take on an importance in direct relation to his goal.

The first thing to do is to simplify the outing. It is necessary, then, to carry as few things as possible and, consequently, "to choose." These material preparations eliminate the idea of flight. But since the instinct which urges flight exists, it is this instinct itself that excites a very active interest in the preparations. Step by step the response arises and the reasoning functions from cause to effect.

Let the teacher not lose sight of the fact that the goal sought is not an immediate one—not the hike—but is rather to make the spiritual being which she is educating capable of finding his way by himself.

To understand the importance of these exercises, which ought to permit social experiences, we must not be satisfied to consider the children's outing a simple health-giving exercise. It is designed to bring the child's attainments to life for him. It is only thus that their realities will penetrate him. That is what we call experience.

A child enclosed within limits however vast remains incapable of self-evaluation and will not succeed in adapting himself to the outer world. For him to progress rapidly, his practical and social lives must be intimately blended with his environment. A general objection may be made that the child's schedule is already too crowded to introduce activities of a practical nature. This is an error, because it is a great deal more tiring to employ only half the faculties nature has bestowed on us. It is as though one were to walk on only one foot on the pretext that using both would be twice the work. Knowledge and social experience must be acquired at one and the same time.

The outing whose aim is neither purely that of personal hygiene nor that of a practical order, but which makes an experience live, will make the child conscious of realities. It is up to the teacher to arrange that the moral teachings of life are sought through social experiences.

Morals have at the same time a practical side, which governs social relations, and a spiritual side, which presides over the awakening of conscience in the individual.

It is difficult to make social relations real if one uses only the imagination; practical experience is necessary. One cannot awaken the conscience by talking about it. The child must exercise a constant watch over his own activities. Thus educational problems can be resolved by means of play when education seeks to resolve them by means of acts.

As walking entails the use of more than just the feet, it is necessary to assist one's step, to render it agile and able to function at its optimum. Let us not forget that these purposeful efforts will affect one's knowledge of the world.

Thus, when we are climbing, if all we think about is putting one foot before the other, fatigue will overtake us long before we reach our goal. But if we walk in a group, happy at the thought of the marvelous view we will surely discover up there, we will reach the summit without fatigue and will benefit in both joy and health. We have been morally conscious of our effort.

This act of consciousness did not cause any additional fatigue. Bring the child to the consciousness of his own dignity and he will feel free. His work will no longer weigh him down.

In the Netherlands five-year-old children ride bicycles on the streets. Swimming ought also to be taught. When one begins to leave the house it becomes necessary to think of one's personal defense. One has to prepare oneself, train oneself, and acquire new skills. It is also necessary to learn to take care of one's clothes, to see that all is in order, to learn to sew on buttons, to remove spots, et cetera. We have prepared material to that end consisting of various textiles such as wool, silk, linen, cotton, et cetera, which we have soiled in different ways. The children are very interested in this exercise. The older children will not only learn to do all these things but they will also get the idea that before going out they ought to see that all their attire is in perfect order.

An individual who is not accustomed to allowing a spot to remain on his clothes will clean them immediately should they become soiled. He possesses a special sensitivity, an active sensibility which had to be developed. A child educated in this way knows how to recognize persons having this sensitivity. This causes him to develop the sense of caring about the correctness of his own person and constant self-inspection. He does not wish to have any trace of disorder on his person, nor does he wish to leave any trace of disorder in his wake.

Another useful exercise is to wrap packages. In order to make a nice package one must first of all take measurements and work methodically. One also needs to know how to prepare and pack what is required for a meal outdoors (plates, glasses, utensils, et cetera).

It is also very important for the child who goes out to know how to orient himself in the field, to recognize the position of the sun, the cardinal compass points, how to guess the approximate time of day, et cetera. We have him observe, for example, that moss is found mainly on the north side of trees in a forest. We have him predict the weather from the clouds and study the direction of the wind. All these things arouse his attention and become actual knowledge. When the children begin to become interested in these things they talk about them to their juniors, thereby handing down their own riches. In this way, when the older ones go out they carry with them knowledge and civilization, which is to say, progress. And a better atmosphere is created around them.

All these activities constitute a symbol of life. Since life outdoors differs from life in a closed environment, a guide and an aim are necessary. In short, to go out, one must be ready for it.

If we would have the same concept for the second period as for the first, we would need to let the child go, to go where he would. At first he will get lost.

Previously, the perfect teacher was one who allowed the child to act, effacing herself. This procedure is not applicable now. The second-period child is living two parallel existences, his home existence and his existence in society. This is new. The scouts introduce some useful elements here. When they go hiking they do exercises conducive to agility. Practical experience is also useful at this age. The children, when hiking, observe the objects left for a purpose by those who preceded them; these signs along the route help them to find their way. Also, the groups who follow separately learn to recognize, by the position of a given object considered as a signal, the direction they themselves must take. This is an active exercise that habituates the children to observe, to seek. This method is altogether different from that which consists of walking with a child while holding him by the hand.

Another scout activity is that of studying animal tracks. We made the very small children notice the smallest details of the environment. It was in this way that they learned to move dexterously, to touch objects without causing them to fall, without breaking them, et cetera. Likewise, now the more evolved child ought to develop the habit of observing all in his universe. The choice of exercises is a function of his age. There are considerations of a physical nature which must take first place in making the choice. The exercises pertaining to movement are dictated more by the age of the child than by the level of his intelligence.

An example: A young child in a school in the Netherlands knew how to do the square of the binomial. This would compare to the knowledge of children much older. But one day, having obtained permission of his teacher to collect spent matches in the forest with his playmates, he did not behave differently from the other children. Like them, he was only occupied with knowing who would find the most, without thinking about the explanations being given by his teacher elsewhere. His concentration on what he was doing gave his age away. A small child still interests himself in little things even though his intelligence is capable of bounding toward much more advanced concepts. One could say that even though a child can escape on the intellectual plane, on the practical plane he remains tied to his age.

5

The Passage to Abstraction —
The Role of the Imagination
as the Door or the Key to Culture

The Passage to Abstraction —
The Role of the Imagination
as the Door or the Key to Culture

WHEN ONE thinks about preparing children to go out of the closed environment where they have been educated up to the age of seven years, a vast panorama comes to mind. To go out of a classroom to enter the outside world, which includes everything, is obviously to open an immense door to instruction. The event is comparable to the appearance of Comenius' *Orbis Sensualium Pictus* in the history of pedagogy.

Before Comenius, scanty knowledge was passed on by the exclusive use of words. Comenius conceived of offering the universe to children by means of pictures—and it seems that it was the initial building block of a new method of education. The amount of knowledge must have increased greatly because of this.

He assembled a book of pictures representing everything that makes up the world: plants, animals, rocks, peoples, geographic maps, historic facts, industry, commerce, medicine, sanitation, the production of the first machines, the way in which they functioned, et cetera, each idea being represented by an image and a brief commentary in words. It seemed easy for the mind to embrace everything looking at the images in the book. It was really a first example of what later became an encyclopedia, except that the encyclopedia returned to the use of the word while *Orbis Sensualium Pictus* remains just about unique in the history of pedagogy.

And yet the idea has remained. We have begun to teach by using tangible objects adapted for handling. But just as ideas lose strength in becoming widespread, the method of Comenius —who knew everything—was weakened by the teacher who presented only her meager knowledge put into pictures.

Also, it is understandable that representation in only two dimensions is insufficient for the child's comprehension. The child is given so little knowledge of nature. But to overcome the difficulty of procuring and preserving objects, we have placed them in museums. Every self-respecting modern school must have a museum. In this way the enclosed objects may be found near the confined children. The adult, underestimating the intelligence of the child, surrounds him with a depressing atmosphere, while what he needs is to *see* things in order to understand them. The capacity of childhood intelligence remains unsuspected. What we hope—we to whom the child has revealed the power of his intelligence—is to revive the idea of Comenius by bringing the world itself to the children.

When the child goes out, it is the world itself that opens to him. Let us take the child out to show him real things instead of making objects which represent ideas and closing them in cupboards.

In its entirety, the world always repeats more or less the same elements. If we study, for example, the life of plants or insects in nature, we more or less get the idea of the life of all plants or insects in the world. There is no one person who knows all the plants; it is enough to see one pine to be able to imagine how all the other pines live. When we have become familiarized with the characteristics of the life of the insects we see in the fields, we are able to form an idea of the life of all other insects. There has never been anyone who has had all the insects of the universe available to his view. The world is acquired psychologically by means of the imagination. Reality is studied in detail, then the whole is imagined. The detail is able to grow in the imagination, and so total knowledge is attained. The act of studying things is, in a way, meditation on detail. This is to say that the qualities of a fragment of nature are deeply impressed upon an individual.

After seeing a river or a lake, is it necessary to see all the rivers and lakes of the world to know what they are? The imagination, afterward, is able to form a concept of the world. A machine, a man who fishes, a man who works—these are all details that go to form knowledge. This is a universal means of learning. It is self-evident that the possession of and contact with real things bring with them, above all, a real quantity of knowledge. The inspiration engendered by it revitalizes the intelligence that was interested and wished to know. Now, from all these things new intellectual interests arise (climates, winds, et cetera). Instruction becomes a living thing. Instead of being illustrated, it is brought to life. In a word, the outing is a new key for the intensification of instruction ordinarily given in the school.

There is no description, no image in any book that is capable of replacing the sight of real trees, and all the life to be found around them, in a real forest. Something emanates from those trees which speaks to the soul, something no book, no museum is capable of giving. The wood reveals that it is not only the trees that exist, but a collection of lives. And this earth, this climate, this cosmic power are necessary for the development of these lives. The myriads of lives around the trees, the majesty, the variety are things one must hunt for, and which no one can bring into the school.

How often is the soul of man—especially that of the child— deprived because one does not put him into contact with nature.

And when this contact is considered, it is only for reasons of health. How could a child describe the difference in nature as seen in daylight and as seen at night when, in our time, he must inexorably go to bed in the evening?

I heard a comment from the mouth of an eight-year-old child which profoundly impressed me: "I would give anything to be able, one night, to see the stars." He had heard them being discussed but he had never seen them. His parents thought it necessary not to allow the child to stay up a single evening on any pretext whatever. All that hygiene, centered on the physical person, has made the world neurotic. It is noted that mental health has diminished in spite of the progress which improves physical health. If tension among adults has increased abnormally, it is because they have formed an erroneous idea of life. These prejudices create many obstacles in the intellectual life of the child. What harm would come from allowing a child to rise later if, as an exception, he were to be allowed to satisfy the interest he takes in discovering the stars or the sounds of the night? The mind of the child is found to be at this age on an abstract level. He is not satisfied with the mere collection of facts; he tries to discover their causes. It is necessary to make use of the psychological state, which permits the view of the thing in its entirety, and to let him note that everything in the universe is interrelated. Thus when the child wants to understand everything, the world, which he has before him, can fill that need.

But it is not always as easy to present the whole as it is to present a detail. But then does it not suffice for the teacher to limit herself to loving and understanding the child? The child must first love and understand the universe. She must therefore prepare herself and the work. Certainly the child is still central. But the teacher must now appeal to that part of the child which finds itself in the world of the abstract. When the child was very small it was enough to call him by name for him to come back. Now we must appeal to his soul. To speak to him is not enough for this; it is necessary to interest him. What he learns must be interesting, must be fascinating. We must give him grandeur. To begin with, let us present him with the world.

In Genesis it says: "God created the heavens and the earth." It is a very simple statement but it has grandeur, and the mind stays awake. When details are presented as being parts of a whole, they become interesting. The interest increases in proportion to the gain in knowledge. In addition, the knowledge presented now must not be on the same scale as before. It must not be purely sensorial anymore. Now the child must have constant recourse to his imagination. Imagination is the greatest force of this age. Since we are unable to present everything, it is up to the child to use his imagination. The instruction of children from seven to twelve years of age must appeal to the imagination. A configuration of reality must evolve in the imagination. It is necessary therefore to be strictly precise. Exactness, as a numeral and as all that makes up mathematics, will serve to build that configuration of reality. Now what is it that strikes the imagination? Above all, grandeur and, next, mystery. The imagination is able to reconstruct the whole when it knows the real detail.

Imagination was not given man for the simple pleasure of phantasizing any more than were the four characteristics common to man (language, religion, death rites, and arts) given to let him live on contemplation. Imagination does not become great until man, given the courage and strength, uses it to create. If this does not occur, the imagination addresses itself only to a spirit wandering in emptiness.

Obstacles abound in the world. But man's mental life gives him the strength to surmount them to accomplish his task. Love of the homeland is based on imagination. Is it not that which gives us the idea of what our country, whose citizens we are, is? Our fight on behalf of children also needs imagination, because we ourselves know only very few children.

The homeland, like the children we thus imagine, does indeed exist and we know it.

He who does not possess the world of the imagination is poor. But the child with too much fantasy is a disturbed child. We do not know how to calm him. We do not say: "Let us suppress the imagination of that child's mind," but rather: *"The child's imagination is insufficient for his mind."* We must nourish the other facet of his intelligence, that which has to do with the external world and his activity. It is in this way that we will discipline him.

The child's imagination is vague, imprecise, without limits. But from the moment he finds himself in contact with the external world *he requires precision*. The requirement is such that the adult would be unable to bring it about. Its full potential lies within the child. When a child's interest is aroused on the basis of reality, the desire to know more on the subject is born at the same time. At such a moment exact conclusions may be presented. Children express the desire for conclusions in their own way. For example, in one of our schools there was once a seven-year-old boy who chose to study the Rhine. The teacher had prepared a map of the river and its tributaries, but the child was not satisfied with it. He wanted to know the relative length of each of the tributaries. (Here we see the idea of mathematics awakened.) He used graph paper to draw a better map. It is in this way that the sense of proportional size and the interest in study are born at the same time. He remained at the same task, by his own choosing, for more than two months. He was not satisfied until he had meticulously completed it. His satisfaction came with his being able to express these concepts in mathematical terms.

Let us draw a parallel here with the smaller children who

by touching objects trained their hands to greater dexterity. The exercise seemed to satisfy something inside of them. Touching for the younger child is what imagining is for the older one. On the former age level we would have worked on the sensorial plane as, for the latter, we work on the level of the imagination. Thus at different levels we encounter parallel phenomena. With the little children the response was infantile. But it is still true that knowledge may truly be developed by awakening the interest. A detail of physics or chemistry is enough to produce the awakening. At the same time, a number of experiments and conclusions arise which bring learning in depth and detail.

The mind bases itself on the imagination, which brings things to a higher level, that of abstraction. But the imagination has need of support. It needs to be built, organized. Only then may man attain a new level. He is penetrating the infinite.

A study outline here presents itself: *to bring the whole by means of the presentation of detail.* Thus, when we wish to consider the study of living beings, the most important thing is first to establish the classification. It has been an error to have sought to suppress it. It has seemed too dry and too difficult, even though it constitutes a precise key for the study of the whole. Not only does the classification help in understanding, but it also aids the memory. Therefore it constitutes a base which one should establish first of all.

Would that the teacher allowed herself to be imbued by the grandeur of this whole to be able to transmit it to the child. It is not only the classification of a few details that must be the point of departure, but the classification of the Whole. And this Whole, emerging at the same time, will serve as the base so that each detail comes to be located in the mind. For example, let us say that the world is the globe on whose surface we live. But let us say immediately that this planet receives reflections from the world of the stars. One cannot, then, isolate it from the whole; one cannot content oneself with observing it all alone. Considered in the abstract, we can envisage it as the empire of three kingdoms—animal, vegetable, and mineral. We show a globe, entirely different from the one used for geography. What is represented in white depicts the land, what is represented in black depicts the water. This globe does not serve in the study of geography, but is intended to stimulate the imagination.

To speak of animals, of vegetables, of minerals is an abstraction. But we will say here: "Man lives in the world and man must conquer it." The intelligence of man must conquer the world as the intelligence of the little child has conquered the environment.

All is strictly interrelated on this planet. And one notes that each science studies only the details of a total knowledge. To speak afterward of the life of man on the surface of the globe is to speak of history. And each detail holds the child's interest by reason of its strict relation to the others. We may examine a tapestry: each detail is embroidery; the whole constitutes a magnificent cloth.

To give the child of seven to twelve years the idea of a whole in nature, for example of the planet on which we live, we must begin by bringing him numbers.

To do well, it is necessary to aim at giving an idea of all the sciences, not in precise detail but only as an impression. The idea is to "sow the seeds of the sciences" at this age, when a sort of sensitive period for the imagination exists. Once the idea has been presented, we must show that a science extends from each branch: minerology, biology, physics, chemistry, et cetera. And, as we have seen, the examination of a detail triggers the study of the whole.

It is understood that one is obliged to begin by the study of a detail. But since nothing exists that does not constitute a part of the whole, it is sufficient to choose one detail at random, which will then become a point of departure in the study of the whole.

6

Water

Water

TO BEGIN, it is necessary to choose an element that is large, even quantitatively, because if an element is present in large quantities its function must be important. Thus, water is one of the most imposing elements of the earth. Let us say at the outset that many animals live in the water, especially in the oceans, and that the animals themselves elicit a great deal of interest. And since imagination could never suffice to give an idea of the number of these animals, the decimal system, by reason of which we may construct enormous numbers, comes to our aid. And mathematics in this way helps the imagination.

In order to form an idea of the quantities, one could say that certain fish deposit 70×10^4 eggs per year. And one could add that other very small animals exist in such great numbers that the largest number a child is capable of writing would not be sufficient. Show these little animals by means of the microscope and say that sometimes a group of them causes a large spot to form on the sea, a spot so large that it would take a ship six days to circumnavigate it. The mind is thus helped more precisely than by simply saying: "This quantity is very large, it is immense."

We have the children note that the beings which live on the land are found only on the surface, while those of which we have just spoken are found throughout the depth of the water; that that depth is often such as to be able to contain the highest mountains. This will help to give an idea of the relationship existing between the beings that live on land and those that live in the seas. The contrast is even greater when one considers that large deserts, almost uninhabited, are found on the land, while the water of the seas abounds in almost all its parts with animals.

What is it that maintains the state of sanitation in the world? If the water of the seas is analyzed, it is found always to be composed in the same manner. The composition may be determined exactly, mathematically. And for how long has the water been of this composition? Always. Why? If it should ever change, even to the minutest degree, all the living beings found there would die.

And there the vital problem of water has been broached.

SUBDIVISION OF THE STUDY OF WATER

Water is very interesting. We need to understand it. Like almost all bodies, it takes three physical states: solid, liquid, and gaseous. Let us emphasize this, because water presents itself to us under these three aspects more commonly than do the others. Even in the solid state it takes various forms (snow, ice), it seems as if by whim. We are able to cause the three forms by means of heat (by cooling or heating it). Since these transformations are so easy to obtain, is it not logical that we use it as our measuring standard? Thus it serves to measure the temperature, and we say: "0° is the point at which water changes to ice. 100° is the point at which water changes to vapor. The interval between these two points is divided into 100 equal parts, thereby giving us centigrade degrees."

We can practically see water transform itself into vapor.

Thus changed, it is much lighter than it was when cooler. It has this in common with the other substances. Only, for water, this is not exact except beginning from 4° above zero. In effect, under 4° it is lighter again. This is a property specific to water. And this is the reason that, in rocks where it has penetrated as a liquid, it increases in volume on cooling and causes them to split just as it causes the pipes of the plumbing to split. Such incidents occur continually in nature. Water therefore continues its work constantly.

This phenomenon is a blessing to the beings that live in water, because if it were heavy in the solid state it would crush them all upon solidifying. Instead, it becomes a veritable protection for them. Let us note that the laws of nature are not absolute. It is necessary that water become lighter upon solidifying, and this occurs contrary to all the laws. If water were an animal, one could say that it acts this way by adaptation. The phenomena of nature are always instructive when examined without prejudice.

When solid substances are introduced into water, only the water evaporates, leaving the solid substances behind. It is in this way that the water evaporated from the seas forms the clouds above the earth and falls again as rain. But the solids it contained are left in the sea. Clouds attract a great deal of interest; their magnificence arouses this interest. And what excites the curiosity especially is that the water in the clouds is in the nonliquid state.

We broach the study of water in the liquid state by beginning with the problem of the rivers which carry solids in suspension to the sea. The water of the rivers is, in fact, abundantly charged with salts. Here again mathematics helps the imagination. To say that the rivers carry an enormous quantity of salts is all right. But to say that the Mississippi alone discharges 70 million kilograms of limestone daily into the sea, and that all the other rivers do likewise in proportion, immediately causes questions like, "Where does all that limestone go? And since when has this been occurring? And how is it that the sea water is not saturated with all that salt? How has it been able to maintain the exact composition necessary for fish life to continue? What happens? Does the material disappear? Is it a miracle?" No. Something happens which permits the earth to continue to exist. And when we see ships sailing on the oceans let us bring our thoughts again to the water in which a continual work is being carried out to maintain the composition intact.*

The idea has been launched. Everything is interrelated and, beginning with a detail, one arrives at the whole by correlation.

Water is also a solvent. Certain substances can be dissolved in it. When they are dissolved they disappear from view (for example, sugar).

The great cosmic function of water is to dissolve rock. It dissolves, in fact, immense masses, equal to mountains thousands of meters high, which we may have imagined to be the most durable materials on earth.

This part of the study of water—the most mysterious because it concerns what the eye does not see—is precisely the one that arouses the most interest. We explain, then, that the water dissolves the limestone contained in the rock. This curious function gives an idea of the immense quantity of limestone existing on the surface of the earth.

In order to realize how much limestone there is, we compare it to a prism with a base twice the size of Europe and 10,000 feet high. Such precise comparisons aid the imagination.

Let us see how the process occurs. The water seizes the limestone, absorbs it, and carries it away. If we do not see this take place it is because the water takes a long time to accomplish its task and we are accustomed to perceive only the work

* The principle of the cosmic theory was inspired by a book well known in Italy: *Acqua ed Aria* by the celebrated geologist Antonio Stoppani.

of a moment. But a number of experiments permit us to establish that the water does indeed act this way—the little holes or pockmarks which may be noted on ancient monuments and the paving stones in parks are similarly marked, et cetera. We shall return to this subject when we discuss the action of water on land.

Water, the great sculptor of rocks, carries substances by various means, including rivers. And if we wish to give an idea of the extent of rivers on the earth, there is no need to make the subject weighty. Let us glance at a map. There we will see that a single river—itself and its tributaries—covers a vast area of the earth. The children are impressed by the great rivers which collect water from all parts of the earth, and which finish in the seas together with all the dissolved substances. We should give many presentations of these rivers. There is no need yet to name the tributaries, but the sight of them stimulates the imagination.

We now cause the children to observe that all the great rivers of the earth spill water and salts into a single ocean, the Atlantic, either directly or by intermediaries in the form of other seas (Arctic Ocean, Mediterranean Sea, et cetera) which are in constant communication with it. And if some great rivers spill elsewhere, into the Pacific for example, little islands form at their mouths, barriers intended to protect the Pacific Ocean. We say, then, that the Atlantic is the collector of all such substances.

We have already mentioned the immense quantity of salts the Mississippi alone carries to the sea. All the other rivers function in a similar fashion. The water subsequently changes to vapor but abandons the substances which it was carrying. Destructive water, a gentle worker, so fresh, works tranquilly. A great quantity of calcareous (chalky) substances remains on deposit at the bottom of the sea. The reason the Atlantic has not been filled by now is that the substances have been distributed into all the other seas. The phenomenon of distribution constitutes another branch of study which may, in part, be included in physical geography (for example, the ocean currents). We will discuss them later.

What is truly impressive is that all the limestone carried to the sea during hundreds of thousands of years has in no way changed the composition of the water. The lives of all the beings that live in the sea depend on this constancy. The cosmic problem therefore consists in causing the evacuation of all that calcium carbonate in order that the water remain unchanged. But how may what is dissolved be eliminated? It is impossible to boil the water of the sea! It is here that another active force intervenes within the sea itself. It is an energy whose task is to fix all the dissolved substances. And this energy is Life. There exist, in fact, live animals that fix the calcium carbonate.

There exist, then, on the one hand, destructive physical forces, and, on the other, live reconstructive forces. From time immemorial there have been animals exercising this function. They are those who dress themselves in shells and who constitute a veritable force charged with the task of seizing the excessive calcium carbonate and fixing it.

The study of aquatic shells is very interesting to children. There are shells so big that a single one of their valves weighs 300 kilograms; there are tiny, microscopic ones—as, for example, the foraminifers—whose fragments may be shown the children under the microscope since they are invisible to the naked eye. They are unicellular beings which form a type of dust comparable to that of the desert. The dust, on collecting, forms calcareous deposits.

The animals having the most important function in this domain are the corals, which have the important property of remaining stationary. While absorbing limestone they multiply and grow until they reach the surface to form islands, vast regions. Indicating on the one hand the existence of rivers on the earth and, on the other, the existence of coral formations, one may discover that these powers have a relation one to the other. One represents the forces that destroy, and the other the energies that simultaneously reconstruct.

The very quantity of the coral islands is an interesting point to bring to the children's attention. Continents are disappearing while others are being constructed. Today we know these islands well, and we may note that in the Pacific they form a continent comparable to Asia. What is curious is that all these constructions are situated in the Pacific Ocean and not in the Atlantic where, in fact, the rivers carry the materials. Let us see why.

It is known that the corals need calm and pure water in which to live. The storehouse of the materials required is in the Atlantic. And the beings that use the materials live very far away. This is similar to what occurs in industry (production takes place in one locality and, far away, the men in a quieter locality use the products). It is a marvelous organization that places the production or storehouse in one place and the consumption and reconstruction elsewhere. Who then transports the substances so far to the immobile corals? The means of communication must exist, as must the means of distribution of these important materials (precisely as for the distribution and transport of industrial products). So we begin to see the living organization, mysterious in itself, but simple to understand. We touch on *physical geography;* on *zoology,* to explain the function of life in the universe; on *mineralogy;* also on certain principles of *physics,* referring to the properties of water; and also on elements of *chemistry,* to explain how water is able to destroy rocks.

All these elements form parts of a whole, intensely interesting as a story. They will tell us the History of the Earth.

A classification of shells is often given. But there are such a great variety having names so difficult that it seems impossible to consider the imposition of this study as sufficiently important to the children. Now, what must immediately be given the children is not the description of all the shells—univalves, bivalves, et cetera—but rather the idea of the immense variety of forms taken on by nature. What strikes the imagination is this, as well as the esthetic talents of the creatures, which do not merely cover themselves with shells for the sake of covering themselves but design those shells in various forms, adorn the designs in a great diversity of ways, each species being different from the others, just as man does not construct his house while thinking only of sheltering himself. We attract the child's attention to the work of life. That is what is important. If the animals were endowed with intelligence and were able to discern an aim in their work, doubtless they would think: "We work to maintain the purity of the oceans; and we exert considerable effort in order to carry away all the calcium carbonate which, without us, would provoke the death of all the seas' inhabitants." But they would not be able to imagine that they are the builders of new lands, of new chains of mountains, and that it is they who form the islands on which new creatures will establish themselves. The real aim of living beings is, in fact, far removed from the apparent one. It would seem at first glance that their function is to seek the best, the happiest conditions of existence. Corals could then be thought to be seekers of a good time. It is indeed curious to see how they strive to live well, seeking a certain temperature, assuring themselves of water that contains much chlorine; they live in salubrious surroundings (as we do when we go to live in the country) far from the agitated and filthy things which are the rivers arriving from the land. It matters little to them that it is the rivers that bring the materials for their use. They try to be as far removed from them as possible in splendid locations, temperate and healthy. They wish to live hygienically. But their work—which is essential—consists in absorbing the water, appropriating the calcium carbonate, and releasing purified water. All the beings that secrete have the same aim. The quantity of water absorbed by them is considerable. It equals, in proportion, the absorption by a man of thirty liters of water per second.

The corals work at such a pace that they need help. To that end there are little algae which work constantly to furnish them with oxygen. One may compare the corals to the masters of servants. It would seem that we have to do with fantastic tales. And yet, all this is reality—but reality that ought to satisfy the imagination.

The corals remain stationary. Someone is needed who will carry them the requisite calcium carbonate. So we discover a vast communications organization (an important chapter which corresponds in human society to the means for commercial communications). We come, in this way, to marine and submarine currents. Let us look at them on the map. They are the means of communication between two oceans.

The movement of water, certainly complicated, is dependent upon a large number of factors (many of which are cosmic). But the currents are not sufficient to create the movement necessary to deliver the calcium carbonate to the secreting animals. We must, therefore, consider also the movement of the animals. Interest brings us immediately to the higher animals, the fish which occur in infinite variety but whose general type may be described thus: two great masses of muscle which move, much as a spoon moves the sugar at the bottom of a cup, without ever stopping.

We may therefore examine two large groups of animals, the heavy secreters that remain on the bottom of the sea without ever, or almost ever, moving, and the fish that move continually. The latter have a light skeleton which barely suffices to support the muscles of movement.

The infinite variety of fish forms a group having particular social relationships. Let us, then, study the lives of fish in the seas.

The life of a fish is very interesting. And what is more interesting yet is the perpetual movement whose cosmic purpose is to move the water. And how pleasant this movement makes the life of the fish! ("Happy and free as a fish in water.") It is important to note that the fulfillment of a great work brings with it the happiness of the living beings who are charged with it. But one may hardly express this idea without the logic of it becoming obvious. To accomplish a great work it is necessary, in fact, to be situated in the best possible conditions.

It is difficult to study the various ocean currents. But it is easy to look at them traced on a chart. And we may tell the children that immense rivers exist not only on land but also in the oceans.

How is it possible to have water currents in water? For the sea is furrowed with currents. One could apply oneself to a sort of anatomical study of the ocean to know exactly the routes of such currents.

The water of the ocean also has its exact, eternal laws. One current always goes in the same direction while another current goes in another direction. And the study of these currents reveals the existence of those found at greater depths. There are exterior factors (such as the temperature, the sun, the attraction of the sun and the moon) and interior factors at the basis of the movement. Among the interior factors is the work of the animals to attract the water down from the surface and to cause it to rise again. One could also compare this circulation with that of blood in the body of an animal. The impure blood goes to the lungs where it is purified and returns pure. Likewise, the secreting animals of which we have spoken represent the lungs of the ocean. They purge the water of the calcium carbonate which it contains and they do this without ever stopping. The process is carried out on a large scale, as if the earth were a living person. This idea remains indefinite in the imagination of the child but it corresponds to reality. Given that each of the details is later studied, it causes him to remember this view of the whole. So the knowledge, carrying its conclusions, radiates as though from a center, much as a seed develops, little by little.

The study of streams on the surface brings us to geography. The streams, red on the map if warm, blue if cold, are easily located by the child. He may be helped by our telling him that each of the currents is an enormous river carrying a quantity of water corresponding to a thousand Mississippi and Amazon Rivers combined. We follow, for example, the equatorial current from the Gulf of Mexico. When it separates, one of its branches forms the Gulf Stream and the other returns in part until it completes the loop. The movement of the currents may be compared to the exercises of practical life. As when one sweeps a room, all the sweepings are accumulated in one corner before being picked up, so here the calcium carbonate disappears. At the extremity of the loop a collector is in fact to be found, the Sargasso Sea.

Because the currents cause a circular movement, it may be noticed that objects are thrown out on the tangent. The objects are thrown out by centrifugal force (for example, pieces of wood and even whole trees) and the routes taken by them are always the same. The hard work of the water always carries the flotage to the same places. This is why, even though no vegetation exists in the frozen regions, a quantity of pieces of wood may be found there. They are used by the inhabitants to build whole cities, and to provide heat for themselves. These anecdotes are as interesting to the children as fables.

Let us keep our eyes on the map an instant longer. It is necessary to expose things to children for sufficient time to attract their attention. Since they assimilate the environment by instinct, they assimilate at the same time that which we have put out. Each applies himself to the work that he has chosen.

But the map remains in place. It interests the child. We note that the currents are all parallel in the Pacific, which is warm. Elsewhere, on the other hand, their courses are tortuous.

By visual observation of the currents it may be concluded that cold water is denser and sinks, while warm water, being lighter, rises. Also, the water purified of calcium is lighter than that which has not yet been purified and it rises to the surface.

The anecdote of the bottle containing a note, thrown into the sea by a shipwrecked person at the tip of Cape Horn and found in Ireland, is a proof of the movement of water.

Certainly one would like to be able to penetrate the mysteries and the majesty inherent in water. In this way the desire to celebrate it in verse is also born. Its mode of action, its intelligent aim, its grandiose mission cause its maternity to be suspected. Is it not, in fact, the mother of all these living beings, the agents of Creation? Saint Francis of Assisi understood this well for, in an outburst of fraternal love for the elements, he sang the praises of "Sister Water who is very useful and humble and precious." It is loved by all because all living beings—plants and animals—are thirsty and cannot live without it. Why would we not admire it and feel gratitude for it as well as the desire to make its acquaintance? The study of water, then, can become a passion, and the precise conclusions reached by a direct acquaintance with it elucidate such a study.

We now look at water from a different point of view. We have already spoken to the child of its property as a solvent and we have seen that its great cosmic function is to dissolve rock. We therefore consider water to be a dissolver. That is already something precise. We now consider the mechanism of this property, which brings us quite naturally to chemistry.

We say that water, in its quality as a "solvent," becomes a "solution." We show that its power to dissolve has very well-defined limits which may be measured. Here the mathematical factor again comes into play. We describe the water that remains at the surface as being "saturated," and we indicate that the surplus forms a "deposit." We then mix another well-known substance, starch, into the water and show that, even in small quantities, starch is not soluble. It mixes but it never dissolves. We then say that the starch remains "in suspension," and we have just used another precise term. Following this, we put a pebble into water to see that it does not dissolve.

Water is nevertheless an excellent solvent. While it is true that there are certain substances it cannot dissolve, it is curious that those it does dissolve are harbored passively. Now, its greatest thirst is for rock and it has never ceased to devour it. It travels to the depths of the earth in its search. Then why is it that the pebble we put into water did not dissolve? Whatever may the mystery be? Something a little different requiring a complementary explanation must be lurking here. Not only does water dissolve solid substances but it also dissolves certain gases, in particular carbon dioxide. This gas is expelled by all animals and the earth itself emits it continually. Water, before it can act on rock, must be charged with this gas which is therefore also found to subsist in the ocean.

Since water is unable, alone, to carry rock away, it first transforms it by means of this gas. What we wish to say is that the rock is first made friable, then it is carried away by the water.

The transformations are different from those that one obtains by means of a simple solution. Water, as is learned in chemistry, works on the rock by an action that is both physical and chemical at the same time.

We show a bottle of water that contains a large quantity of carbon dioxide under pressure—in other words, a supersaturated solution of carbonic acid. Water that penetrates the earth may also contain a large quantity of this gas precisely because it is under pressure. This is what happens when it digs underground galleries and wells. But when the water comes out of the earth it restores all the surplus of calcium carbonate which it possesses under pressure. It is at this time that it produces the large mineral formations on the surface of the earth. Tufa and travertine are two examples of this. The action is comparable to that which occurs when a bottle under pressure allows carbon dioxide to escape and the pressure to fall when it is opened.

The water therefore has gone underground where it has charged itself with rock which it carries to the surface and deposits. The rock like a veritable mason, will form constructions.

Water is active, has a hearty appetite, and is capable of containing an enormous quantity of this gas for which it is avid and which is its collaborator in the important work of devouring the rock. This is why, during heavy rains, the water, which falls more charged with carbon dioxide than it was as a vapor, leaves its traces on the rock.

7

Some Chemistry Experiments

Some Chemistry Experiments

FROM OUR examination of the currents on the maps we have given the child the idea that some liquids are heavier than others and that the lighter liquids lie over the heavier ones. We now reach certain conclusions obtained by means of exercises that will teach the technical and scientific terms, even some having no connection with those used for the currents. These exercises are parallel to those of practical life which helped the children in learning to make precise movements. Thus, the use of test tubes and funnels constitutes a new manual exercise for the new stage. Certain actions are comparable to those the child performs when he pours water into a glass. But here even more attention is required because the container is smaller.

Let us, then, pour liquids of different weights into a test tube —the term "specific weight" is here introduced. The best way to understand this term is to see the strata of the different liquids: at the bottom we have mercury; we pour water in next, then oil, and finally methyl alcohol. In order to identify them better, we color each of the liquids differently.

Taking two test tubes, we put water and crystallized sugar in one, water and starch in the other.

The sugar crystals dissolve slowly, so that we could doubt their solubility in water. But if we apply heat, the sugar soon

Figure 1.

disappears. In place of a *cold solution* we obtain a *warm solution*.

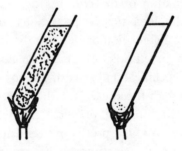

Figure 2.

These operations, fascinating to little children, require nevertheless a certain attention. We are giving them practical information—that sugar crystals are soluble in warm water and not soluble in cold water—at the same time that we are training their patience.

As for the starch, it remains undissolved even after shaking the tube. Its presence makes the water opaque: it is "in suspension."

Therefore, a solution may be colored but remain transparent whereas the liquid containing a substance in suspension becomes opaque. The two test tubes just prepared show this clearly.

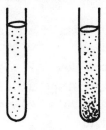

Figure 3.

We now take a blue solution of copper sulfate and water to see if it is possible to free the water of the dissolved substance. In order to filter it, we must first see how to prepare a filter in a funnel, how to attach the paper, and how to measure to prevent the paper being too large for the funnel. The paper must not reach the funnel's rim. For the experiment to be more striking, we first filter the water containing starch. We see that it becomes clear again. We have, in this way, demonstrated the ease with which water may be freed of a substance it contains in suspension. We proceed in the same way with the solution of copper sulfate. We note that the water, although filtered, remains colored. This means that the solution is a liquid that has itself become a new substance.

We have seen that, upon filtering a liquid in which a substance is found to be in suspension, that liquid becomes clear. And yet the substance found in [dissolution] has not been removed. To remove it, we must boil it. If we do not have the apparatus necessary for distillation we cannot succeed in purifying the water. But we are able to see what remains of the dissolved substance when we have caused the water to evaporate. This operation is called "calcination." We recall the calcium carbonate that remains on the bottom of the sea after the evaporation of the water.

On the other hand, if a deposit remains in the test tube, we are able, though imperfectly in practice, to free the liquid from the deposit by "decantation." These new terms are exact, and we will be able to write them in a book or on separate cards with an explanation of each.

We have the children note that to boil liquids we always place a screen between the flame and the flask, which indicates that great care must be taken in order not to burn it when the liquid is entirely evaporated.

This experiment shows that the water has disappeared without having been able to take anything with it. The copper sulfate that remains is a solid which we may remove and again dissolve in water to obtain a second solution as blue as the first. Thus we have been able to remove the substance first found in water and put it into other water.

These exercises are very simple but they require time because it is necessary to wait patiently while the liquids settle, while substances dissolve, or while the liquids evaporate. Calm and attention are also required. The psychological effect produced on the children at this age may be compared to that of the silence lesson on the younger children. The small children severely restricted their movements, while the older ones must measure their movements and must therefore pay concentrated attention to them.

We may follow now with another exercise which is neither complicated nor difficult to understand but which requires patience, care, and a steady hand. It consists in filling a test tube with water. When the tube is full to the brim it may be noted, on careful observation, that the surface of the water is concave because the water adheres to the glass. This union is called "cohesion." More difficult yet is the task of adding a small quantity of water to the test tube which is already full. When this has been done it will be seen that the surface of the water has become convex. This penomenon is caused by the powerful force of cohesion of the water itself. It is for this reason that falling water takes the form of drops—i.e., a spherical form. The drop is simultaneously convex and concave.

We can have the children recall the formation of stalactites and stalagmites. These also fix the children's attention on water.

Let us bring them to discover, through experiment, the principle of communicating receptacles.

We take a U-shaped test tube and explain that the water may come to the surface of the land because it seeks the level of the underground water table. Many springs are the result of the existence of this phenomenon. Thus, to use on one hill the water whose source is on another hill of the same altitude, it is enough to put them in communication. If the Romans had known this principle they would not have built the immense aqueducts we admire. It would have been sufficient for them to connect one point with the other.

Then, too, we have them note that the surface of the water is a horizontal plane. To show this we take a V-shaped test tube. In the oblique arm, the form of the surface of the water is elliptic. In the other, held vertically, the surface is circular. This proves that the surface of a liquid always remains on the horizontal plane. In fact, to find the horizontal, it suffices to let liquid come to rest. From these demonstrations arise principles which allow us to introduce mathematical determinations when we later broach the study of scientific instruments.

We speak now of the chemical composition of water. The child needs to know something of science which has, in our day, taken on such great importance. We cannot yet give him the great theories or the exact chemical science; that will come later. But at this age he must receive the seeds which will germinate later. He needs an impression, an idea which above all awakens interest. If he acquires the interest he will later be able to study and understand these subjects rapidly. If the interest is not aroused, the sciences, which have attained such a degree of development and which have so much influence on present-day civilization, will remain obscure.

We must hunt, therefore, for everything that may be accessible to the mind of the child in order to create the bases for future development. That is to say, that we must sow impressions before presenting science. We must here again have recourse to the imagination to create the impressions and to reach conclusions little by little. To do this we must seek the symbols accessible to the child that bait the primitive logic that makes him reason. Nothing can speak to his imagination better than science, because he sees in it a sort of magic. The fact that a body in association with another—as in the case of water—may invisibly form a third really gives the impression of something magic. The mind awakens in the face of creation.

Hydrogen, the light, invisible gas which seeks to escape, and oxygen, another gas which is always contained in the air—both of which we never see, but which are necessary to us and of which the children have always heard—are breathed by all, even the fish in water. Oxygen is a surprising gas. It is because of it that things burn.

Air is made up of about four-fifths oxygen and about one-fifth nitrogen, which moderates the oxygen. Without it, the oxygen would burn everything. We know nitrogen. We have often heard about nitrified substances. During the war Germany used the nitrogen of the air to obtain explosives. It is curious to note that one gas of which the air is made up burns and that the other explodes. What is more, oxygen and hydrogen unite to give us water.

8

Carbon in Nature

Carbon in Nature

THE PURE air we breathe is soiled by carbon dioxide emitted by the lungs. Carbon dioxide is poisonous to us and to animals. How is it that we have never been asphyxiated? This is another mystery much like that of water. There is an element that maintains the purity of the air and has done so for centuries and centuries since the beginning.

It could be supposed that only hydrogen and oxygen, both invisible, existed; that an explosion occurred; that the cataracts of heaven were opened; and that water had been created. Water is formed of two parts hydrogen and one part oxygen. The water which did not exist before could have been formed suddenly by a spark. It is in fact possible to make water in this way. These experiments should not be done too soon. But the phenomenon may be described as though it were a marvelous tale by explaining how water, which may be seen and felt, is formed by two substances both of which are invisible.

And while we are on the subject of the creation of a substance, we inform the child that chemistry is the study of newly created substances. To illustrate, we place a piece of sugar in a flask, pour on it a liquid having the appearance of water— sulfuric acid. We mix the two substances well. The sugar dissolves in the water. We suddenly see smoke come from the flask. We are present at the formation, as if by magic, of a new substance: carbon. White sugar is, in substance, a piece of coal. Coal, then, according to its different forms and aspects may have different uses and qualities.

It may be said that all the substances that burn become coal. Trees become coal. The roast forgotten on the fire becomes coal. We, too, are carbon combined with other substances. Coal is found scattered all over. It is a very important substance. The desire to discover certain characteristics of these elements never fails to arise. The small child is already using symbols. The letters of the alphabet are symbols. He has only a small number, but, combined among themselves, they form words, poems. The musical notes are symbols, dots. Music makes us happy, makes us sing and dance. So why would we not be able to symbolize another phenomenon, that of creation?

The four elements we symbolize for the children in this way are, as it were, the key to the universe.

Figure 4.

They are easy to remember because they have 1, 2, 3, and 4 lines. They do, in fact, make us think of keys.

We could depict them in the form of bodies having arms capable of grasping one another. Some elements irresistibly combine (embrace). Thus hydrogen combines with oxygen which, having two arms, is able to hold two hydrogens. Water is represented thus:

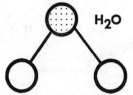

Figure 5.

On the other hand, carbon, which has four arms, uses two of them to attach to each of two oxygens to form carbon dioxide, which is represented:

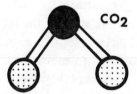

Figure 6.

These two elements are fundamentally important. They could be considered to be the two activators of the universe.

Nitrogen, which has three arms, combines with three hydrogens to form a relatively important compound, ammonia.

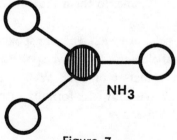

Figure 7.

Ammonia is the ultimate form taken by the nitrified substances of an organism in decomposition.

The way in which the elements unite is what maintains the attention of the child. Here is the symbol for nitric acid:

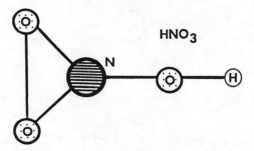

Figure 8.

Since oxygen has two arms, it requires an element that can take them. Thus, two oxygens attach to each other, and the other attaches to hydrogen, while each of the oxygens uses one of its arms to attach to the three arms of a nitrogen. It is quite difficult for us to use ammonia to make nitric acid. But in nature this occurs constantly. It occurs, however, by means of an intermediary such as living beings—microbes, which possess a power we do not have. They separate the hydrogens and replace them with oxygens. If the micro-organisms did not exist, the earth would fill with ammonia and the plants would not find nutrients because they feed on nitrates coming from nitric acid. The micro-organisms, then, contribute to the nutrition of the plants, because it is thanks to them that the chemical transformations take place.

In carbon dioxide, of which we have spoken, it is the carbon that is the principal element. When we spoke of calcium carbonate, it was again a matter of coal. Well, then, are the rocks themselves carbon? We show the formula of calcium carbonate which is depicted thus:

Figure 9.

Carbon, which has four arms, uses two to hold calcium, which has only two, and with each of the other two hands holds an oxygen which uses each free hand to hold the third oxygen.

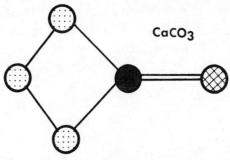

$CaCO_3$

Figure 10.

We now examine the diagram for water. Speaking of water, we remember calcium carbonate. The carbon takes advantage of the opportunity to escape with two oxygens in the form of carbon dioxide. The compound that remains, calcium hydrate, is soluble in water and can be carried away with it.

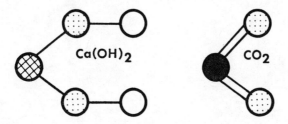

$Ca(OH)_2$ CO_2

Figure 11.

This is the great drama of nature, thanks to which mountains are decomposed and new lands formed. Carbon, calcium, hydrogen, and oxygen form two substances that are in perpetual search for each other. And, at the same time, the opposite is happening because there is always carbon dioxide in the water.

They combine to form calcium carbonate and water again. It is in this way that water dissolves and recreates continuously.

It is interesting to be present at what happens among all these elements which one could consider as the keys that command the intimate movements of nature. If the ideas are brought forward in this simple fashion, it becomes passionately interesting to see what will happen. And once one is acquainted with the substances, one depicts them by means of simple symbols.

9

A Few Ideas of Inorganic Chemistry

A Few Ideas of Inorganic Chemistry

THE POINT of view from which we bring the children to these sciences in their embryonic state must be well understood. Our presentation must be sensorial and imaginative, given by means of clear visual symbols which permit details to be determined.

We are trying to arouse the child's interest. Should we fail to arouse it immediately, we must still trust the same principle while we make our presentations in a specific environment and await the reaction. If the enthusiasm is not manifested we do not delay but proceed. If the enthusiasm is manifested we have an open door. We are at the beginning of a long road. We will travel with the child. But what we would most like to recommend is not to begin too late. Thus, the presentation of chemistry may be made at nine years of age. The interest may even manifest itself sooner.

A question that always exists in our adult minds is whether these problems, which already seem to us to be so difficult, will be well understood by the child. "Will he understand molecules, the atom? Will he understand the formulas?" It seems impossible to us that he will follow the study of atomic theory. But it is not a science we want to bring to him at this time. It is nothing else than a germ capable of arousing interest and which will develop later. We recommend above all not to give too many explanations but rather to specify names. Here is an anecdote to illustrate this advice: A child asks his father why the leaves are green. Happy to seize the opportunity, the father launches into explanations of chlorophyll, the air, light, seeming never to finish. The child listens politely but thinks: "What a shame to have provoked all that!"

As for the question of the molecule and the atom, we can explain it thus: Let us hunt for the smallest part of something. For example, let us divide a geometric figure in other, always smaller figures until we can go no further. The atom is the part of an element that cannot be divided. Here is another comparison: "For humanity, the atom is man. If a man be subdivided he is no longer a man." Going from this example we can say: man and woman are two atoms of humanity. A man and a woman together form a molecule. Which is to say that a molecule is composed of [at least] two parts.

The children, moreover, will not pose these questions merely because it is the symbolic representations that interest them. Rather, what pleases the children about water is that the oxygens and hydrogens wish to remain united and that they seek each other as though driven by a mutual liking for each other. In the same way, carbon unites itself with oxygen to form carbon dioxide.

Hydrogen has only one possibility of uniting, oxygen has two, et cetera. Thus, whether it has 1, 2, 3, or 4 arms, each must seize another element. If the atoms were alone they would unite among themselves so as to be always satisfied. But instead of speaking about "arms," we can now say that the elements have a value of 1, 2, 3, or 4 and that the value is called "valence." Now we say that hydrogen has a valence of 1, that oxygen has a valence of 2, et cetera.

We must have the courage to give as many names as pos-

sible. The more difficult the names are, the more attractive they
are to the child. And then one may say that hydrogen is uni-
valent, that oxygen is bivalent, et cetera. It is easier to express
this concept this way than to speak of 1, 2, or 3 arms.

For all that, it is not in proportion to their valences that
elements unite. They must also have an affinity which causes
them to seek one another. They could be said to have an instinct that pushes them to seek out one rather than another. The
secret is in the choice and not in the valences. For this reason
we cannot play with elements. The symbols show which substances are present and how a compound is formed. In this
way we are brought to write the formula.

When all the valences are saturated, satisfied, the compound
is stable.

Two elements cannot unite unless there is affinity. Thus,
oxygen and nitrogen—both of which have been present in the
atmosphere for centuries and centuries—have not united. It is
as though there were present in the atoms an interior force that
gives them the possibility of choice. The union corresponds to
the power of the valences, which is to say that the characteristics
are proper to the atoms themselves. They are driven to choose,
to form a stable compound that will be a new substance.

Rock is formed of oxygen, carbon, and calcium. And yet
neither marble nor alabaster is oxygen, which is a gas, or
carbon, or calcium. It is another material, a new creation, a
rock.

All of creation—water, rock—derives from the atoms which
seek each other out, unite to each other, and, together, lead to
a new creation. It is always the same elements that seek the
atoms: the same and not others. The limits are ruled by laws.
All the details of creation constitute a marvel which we must
not fail to bring to the children's attention.

Through visual representations of form and color, with the

letters of the alphabet or with musical notes, we bring forward the idea of stability. By the help of experiments we are able to be present at the creation of a substance, as we have seen with the coal. This is something absolutely sensorial which arouses the child's interest. There is no need, at present, to penetrate further into the study of inorganic chemistry, to which the study of all mineral compounds belongs.

10

A Few Ideas of Organic Chemistry

A Few Ideas of Organic Chemistry

WE CAN even bring the child some notions of organic chemistry. This is thought today—but this is a mistake—to be more difficult, so much so that it is not taught before the student's entry into the university. But if some formulas of organic chemistry are presented in visual form, why should they be more difficult than the others?

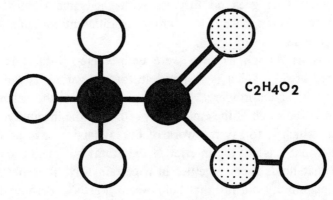

$C_2H_4O_2$

Figure 12.

What, then, is so complicated about this formula, which is that of acetic acid? We can now illustrate also that of butyric acid, which differs from the preceding only in that it has two

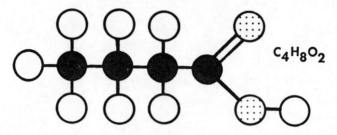

Figure 13.

more carbon brothers. We then proceed to illustrate palmitic acid, which has a long chain of carbon atoms.

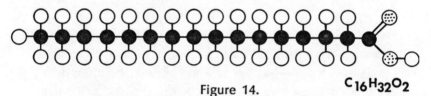

Figure 14. $C_{16}H_{32}O_2$

The OH group is called "hydroxyls."

We note that carbon, which enters into organic compounds, is the vertebral column and that what revolves around it is simply water. One goes no further. With the same elements—hydrogen, oxygen, carbon—a number of different combinations may be made.

It is as though a gown were embroidered with different colored threads. What is responsible for the variety is the ingenuity of the embroiderer. It is less a question of the valences —that is, the stitch of the embroidery—than of the ingenuity, the power, which is to say the work of life. What we have here is the fact that it is not the interior of the atoms but their exterior force that holds them together in a certain way. It is not the chemical affinity but life that holds them together. Perhaps this concept, not the formula, is difficult. The molecules can be very large, so that each molecule may have three hundred or more atoms.

It is necessary to remember the stability of compounds formed, as a family through the centuries, which is a particularity of inorganic chemistry. The particularity of organic chemistry is the instability of the compounds formed. That is to say, these substances are formed by groups of atoms held together by an exterior force in such a way that the atoms are interchangeable but the type of compound persists.

There are other slightly more complicated formulas in which the atoms of carbon are not present as brothers holding hands. We find carbon and the hydroxyls but we also find a novelty: some atoms of oxygen slip in, as, for example, in this formula for starch:

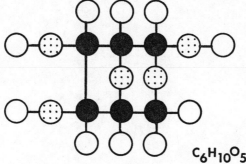

$$C_6H_{10}O_5$$

Figure 15.

and in this one for glucose:

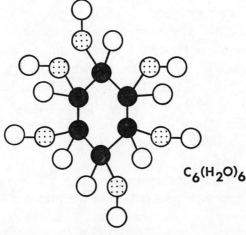

$$C_6(H_2O)_6$$

Figure 16.

Here we have a schematic diagram which may be used as an example of correlation. It is a tree with its root, trunk, branches, and leaves.

Figure 17.

The action of which we have already spoken takes place in all its parts. The tree, in fact, takes its nourishment from the ground through its roots. Chemistry permits us to discover that the roots of the tree absorb nutritive substances, of which water and nitrogen are the two main ones. But the nitrogen, in order to constitute a nutritive substance, must be found in a special chemical composition. This poses problems. What is it that furnishes the nitrogen which the plants require continually and which they absorb? What or who replaces this nitrogen in the ground? Nothing in nature may be touched upon without this problem arising.

All living beings need something or someone to help them to live. And here rises before us the problem of the secret of nature, so important in education.

The organic substances that are no longer alive fall to the ground. If the organic substances are no longer alive, the force that maintained the atoms together as molecules no longer exists. So the molecules break up, the atoms detach and follow their instincts: carbon takes two oxygens away with it, et cetera.

In this way the organic compounds become inorganic. Very little remains of the living beings: a little carbon dioxide, a little ammonia, and a little water. The organic substances disappear. All this work of disintegration takes place in the ground in infinitely small reactions.

One day in Rome I was present at the exhumation of the remains in a paupers' cemetery, an operation which takes place every ten years in order to reclaim space. I saw the workers dig without finding more than the occasional bit of débris. They were digging in beautiful black, clean soil, a good, healthy, odorless soil.

Plants absorb these nitrified organic substances from the earth through the roots. Ammonia remains behind. The plants cannot absorb it in this form. It is necessary, then, for the compounds of nitrogen and hydrogen to change to compounds having oxygen. This is very difficult to reproduce in chemistry. In nature, microbes in the ground devote themselves to this task continually. From this work arise the nitrites and nitrates which the plants can absorb. Without the microbes this passage from death to life would not exist. When all the organic substances have disappeared, carbon dioxide, water, and nitrogen remain. The nitrogen is changed and the plants may then absorb it.

Green leaves are found at the other end of the tree. The substance responsible for their color is called chlorophyll. The role of chlorophyll is to absorb carbon dioxide—a poison continually emitted by all animals and even by the earth—from the air and to decompose it: to retain the carbon and to allow the oxygen to escape. The tree thus becomes a veritable storehouse of carbon. We know this is so because we use wood to obtain warmth. We also know that tree fossils constitute store-houses of carbon. This is why leaves are necessary for the absorption of carbon and the purification of the air.

But chlorophyll all alone would not be able to complete this task. Collaboration is necessary in the form of the sun's rays. Even the tree would not be able to accomplish its great task alone if it were not for the other force independent of it—solar energy.

The tree then is a link, on the one hand to invisible microbes, and on the other hand to the sun. Many good and beautiful things owe their existence to the contact with microbes: flowers and fruits . . . How generous the tree is! How hard it works! It prepares carbon. It purifies the air. It gives us fruit. It gives us flowers. All the plants cause this thought to arise. Even plants more modest than the tree devote themselves to this useful task and as veritable industries they prepare nutritive substances. We mention potatoes, wheat, starch, beets, sugar cane, et cetera.

That is the nature of creation.

We see that the plants devote themselves to the tasks proper to them just as do the corals that construct a continent. They are workers who draw their nourishment and seek the best conditions of life. That is the cycle of life, as we have seen the cycle of rock. All living beings are destined to contribute to the well-being of other living beings. It is difficult to establish a parallel between the phenomena of nature and those of human life. But a parallel does exist, and principally because men, as a group, must have a great task in creation, although on a level considerably higher than that of nature. Each man works for other men. Industry and commerce may be considered as a relationship comparable to those found in nature. Could we not restudy the history of humanity from this new point of view?

If we examine nature and the supernature constructed by

man side by side, all that belongs to the former elucidates what happens in the latter.

The difference between the constitution of vegetable cells and animal cells may be noted.

Plant cells are rectangular, or, better, prismatic. Their membranes are thick, strong, and only slightly permeable. They give an impression of the strength of vegetables and the power of their defense. Also, as they grow they spread in all directions. They are characterized by branching. Their roots fix themselves in the ground to hold them secure. They absorb the sun's rays, particularly through the leaves. The plant is beautiful and clean. It sports many colors and scents. Its roots transform ugliness into beauty.

Animals begin their cycle as spheroid cells the membrane of which, being very fine, very light, seems to be in continual danger. Timid of aspect, they limit themselves, unlike the plant cells, and do not spread out. As they grow they fold back over themselves in one, two, or more layers. The complexity of their functions is always found on the inside. In addition, the animal is unable to obtain the substances for his nourishment without moving about to procure them.

Which of the two has superior characteristics? The animals are considered to be on a higher level of nature and yet we consider the plants to have superior characteristics. The animals give the impression of being humble, without defense, always moving, buffetted here and there. And yet we say that the animal is superior for that very reason. We call it "animal" because there is something within it that guides it and makes it move. In continual danger, it must always hunt its own nourishment. It depends on the vegetable world, be it for food or for the purification of the air it breathes. It never has the purity of the vegetable, which is always clean. It could be thought that the animal is always in battle against the vegetable, and yet the two forms are necessary to each other and give mutual assistance to each other.

Interest now begins to mount with regard to human behavior. Nature reveals that he who is truly a superior and strong being is he who, in spite of weakness, always gains the upper hand.

11

Conclusion

Conclusion

ALL OF what we have just suggested is, in reality, only an example for the application of the method. But we want the child to penetrate to a higher understanding. What must first be understood is our aim, which is to follow as nearly as possible, as all-inclusively as possible, the needs of growth and of life.

We have touched on several cycles, as, for example, that of calcium carbonate. But all maintains itself. And what is interesting is that we are able to orient ourselves among these correlations. To present detached notions is to bring confusion. We need to determine the bonds that exist between them. When the correlation among the details, by now linked one to the others, has been established, the details may be found to tie together among themselves. The mind, then, is satisfied and the desire to go on with research is born.

Then, finding the correlation between things with the child, thereby obeying the impulse of the human mind, we create a philosophy for him. And why may not the child philosophize?

Since the human mind is mathematical and philosophic, we try, in reasonable proportions, to turn it toward mathematics and philosophy.

Here is an essential principle of education: to teach details is to bring confusion; to establish the relationship between things is to bring knowledge.

APPENDICES

A

Erdkinder

Erdkinder *

GENERAL CONSIDERATIONS:

THE NEED for reform in secondary teaching which makes itself so urgently felt poses not only an educational problem but also a human and social problem, which may be summed up in this way: The schools, such as they are today, are not adapted to the needs of the adolescent or to the age in which we live.

Society, whose complications and contradictions are reaching the bursting point, finds itself having to face a crisis that menaces the peace of the world and civilization itself. The progress made by science and its practical applications, though involved in the crisis, are definitely not the cause. The crisis is due, more than to any other cause, to the disproportion existing between the development of man and that of the exterior world which he has not kept up with.

While extremely rapid material progress has entirely transformed social life, the development of the schools, immobilized at a stage where they did not even correspond to the needs of the past, today presents an absolute contrast with human progress.

Even though secondary-school reform cannot alone resolve

* The Children of the Soil

all the problems of our age, it must constitute a necessary stage and contribute in a practical way, even though incompletely, to the reconstruction of society.

The problem of education today is of a general order of importance. Its solution must aid and protect the development of man. Promoting the betterment of the individual is the way in which education must better society.

The education of adolescents is of capital importance because adolescence is the age when child becomes man, which is to say, a member of society.

If, from the physical point of view, puberty is the transition between childhood and adulthood, it is, from the psychological point of view, a transition between the mentality of the child—who lives in the family—and that of man who must live in society.

The child, from birth to twelve years, has completed a full cycle. From seven to twelve years he has been able, thanks to his freedom and to our behavior with respect to him, to attain a level three years ahead of children from other schools. In addition to intellectual development, our education has brought him the faculty of easy social relations with other individuals.

At this age the child has finished a period of life. Nature makes this obvious. At this time the studies ought to be directed toward humanity, toward human life, and particularly toward the men who have helped civilization advance. Until he is twelve years old, nature ought to constitute the child's primary interest. After twelve years, we must develop in the child the feeling of society, which ought to contribute to more understanding among men and, as a result, more love. Let us develop admiration and understanding for work and for the life of man to this end. We put particular emphasis on the practical exercises (wih soil, gases, et cetera). We have the child participate in social work of some kind. We help him intellectually, by means of study, to fathom man's work in society in order to develop in him the human understanding and solidarity which are so sorely needed today.

When ethics bring to future generations a feeling of attachment, not only to the homeland but to all of humanity, the basis of love and of peace will have been built.

The two new needs of the adolescent—to be protected during the delicate physical transition period, and to be placed in a position to understand the man's role which he will play in society—cause the emergence of two problems of equal importance regarding education at this age.

Let us specify that the social reality of our time that ought to arouse the strongest reactions lies in uncertainty about the future.

In complete evolution, the material world offers uncertainties and dangers due to new adjustments. We have lost the "security" of days gone by. The times when a profession was quietly handed down from father to son are past. The certainty of a good job which rewards diligent study is lost. The family is no longer able to guarantee this as it used to be able to. Neither is the state in condition to assure employment to citizens aiming at higher professions when they come out of specialized schools. We must now face new difficulties to which the insecurity of modern conditions has given rise.

The world is partly in disintegration, partly in reconstruction. The succession of progress and recession creates instability. The world is comparable to terrain being tested by the plow.

Under these social conditions we must remember that the only sure guide for education is the very personality of the children to be educated.

It is necessary, then, to prepare the human personality for unforeseen eventualities and not only to keep in sight the conditions to be foreseen by logic alone. We must develop the possibility of supple and live adaptation without rigid specialization. In the fierce battle which social life has become, man needs a strong character and a fast mind in addition to his courage. He needs to reinforce these principles by moral training and to be endowed with practical capabilities to face up to the difficulties of life.

The faculty of adaptation is essential today. Because if progress continues to open new careers, it also continues to eliminate or to revolutionize traditional employments.

It is not a question of excluding the preparation for the intellectual professions from the secondary schools, and much less one of reducing culture. Education must, on the contrary, be very broad and very complete—not only for those who are to go on to intellectual professions but for all men who live in a time characterized by the progress of science and its applications.

Laborers today need education. They need to understand the complex problems of our times. Otherwise the role that their work plays in the plan of society will be nothing else than that of a pair of ignorant hands. As they are at present, it could be said that they have no head at all, while the intellectuals will remain crippled as long as their hands remain untrained. Their minds will become sterile if they do not become conscious of the magnitude of the practical realities around them.

Men who have hands and no head and men who have a head and no hands are equally out of place in the modern community.

The problem of reform of the secondary school will not be resolved by suppressing "culture," or by losing sight of the need to prepare youth for intellectual professions. But it is essential that this preparation does not lull men to sleep in a false feeling of security and does not make them incapable of facing unforeseen difficulties of reality by leaving them ignorant of the conditions of the world in which they are destined to live.

Not so long ago outdoor sports were introduced into education in order to furnish physical exercise to the young people who lived shut-in and sedentary lives. Today, the need for a more dynamic education of the character and for a clearer consciousness of social reality is making itself felt.

The secondary school, such as it is at present, has no other aim than to prepare the pupils for a career, as if the social conditions of our lives were still peaceful and stable. This school takes no particular care of the personalities of the children, any more than it furnishes the physical care needed in this period of adolescence. Thus, not only does it not correspond to the social conditions of our day, but it is utterly bankrupt before the task it will have to take on: to protect and encourage the blossoming of the personalities of adolescents, the human energy on which the future depends.

The young people are constrained to work by "duty," by "necessity," not by interest. No definite goal that would bring immediate satisfaction and would renew interest for continuous effort is proposed to them.

They are directed by an exterior and illogical force, and the best of their individual energy is wasted. Adolescents and young adults are treated like elementary-school children until their maturity. At fourteen and sixteen years old they are still liable to the petty treatment of "bad marks" with which the teachers weight their work. This method is analogous to that which weighs lifeless objects with the mechanical help of a balance. Work is "measured" as an inanimate object and not "judged" as a product of life. And it is on these marks that the future of the student depends. Under these conditions, studies constitute a crushing burden which weighs on youth while they ought rather to be considered a privilege: the initiation into science, the pride of our civilization. The young adults—the men of the future—are formed in a narrow and artificial mold. What a miserable life is offered them, what a penitence without end, what a futile renunciation of their dearest aspirations!

What is more, the secondary school as it is at present is an obstacle to the physical development of adolescents. The period of life during which the body attains maturity is, in fact, a delicate one: the organism is transformed; its development is rapid. It is at that time so delicate that medical doctors compare this period to that of birth and of the rapid growth of the first years. A particular predisposition for certain illnesses, grouped under the heading "illnesses of the adolescent," is to be ascertained. The predisposition to tuberculosis is one of the principal dangers to which the child is exposed during the transition period of becoming an adult.

This period is equally critical from the psychological point of view. It is the age of doubts and hesitations, of violent emotions, of discouragements. There occurs at this time a diminution of the intellectual capacity. It is not due to a lack of will that there is difficulty in concentration; it is due to the psychological characteristics of this age. The power of assimilation and memory, which endowed the younger ones with such an interest for details and for material things, seems to change.

Now let us examine what happens to an adolescent in the secondary schools: He changes teacher and subject every hour; he changes them without any logical continuity. One cannot adapt one's thoughts to a new subject in an hour. And even should one adapt, another teacher immediately begins another subject. It is in this state of mental agitation that this difficult period of human life elapses. Details, many details, a large number of subjects are touched on—but all in the same superficial manner. Latin is taught, like mathematics, in the same way as religion, even though religion is not a subject similar to the others. It needs special study, just as do the laws governing the construction of society.

Essential things are presently taught at the same level as details. We must bring to the consciousness that which awaits it in life.

Adolescence is characterized by a state of expectation, by a preference for works of creation, by a need to fortify self-confidence. The child suddenly becomes hypersensitive to the sharp, humiliating treatment that he has up to now suffered with patient indifference. And the reactions of bitter rebellion that result sometimes give rise to morally abnormal characteristics. It is at this age that the "sensitive period" that ought to develop feelings of justice and personal dignity occurs. These feelings are the most noble of characteristics and ought to prepare the man to become a social being.

There is considerable transformation. This period has been termed a "renaissance," a veritable second birth. It is, then, a birth to a new life. The individual becomes a social newborn.

It is a social man who does not yet exist but who is already born. Physically, he is still weak and full of newly felt needs. Doctors say that the mortality rate is sufficiently high to be compared to that of infants. But then it is easy to understand that rapid growth can weaken an individual.

A parallel powerful interior development occurs at this time. What is it? A mystery. Just as the newborn's mind is a mystery, so is the social newborn a mystery. Each time we find ourselves before a mystery of creation we must consider that creation is divine. It is not due to the will of the child. A decisive, delicate period, worthy of our respect, presents itself as our responsibility. What is it? We do not know, but we must hasten to find out. It must be the child who reveals to us what happens during the growth which is the real, actual creation of social man. Consequently we must place him in the conditions required for the revelations to occur. Up to the present, the child has remained in the family and at school. We have noted that he does not work voluntarily, that he tires quickly, and that a large number of absences occur at this age.

Since there is a radical change in the person, there must be a radical change in his education.

There are two kinds of difficulty to consider:
1. The difficulties inherent in the present form of society.
2. The difficulties due to the vital needs of the child.

It is not necessary that life remain an "unknown" in which the orphan feels lost, in which the immigrant despairs of finding success because it remains impossible for him to apply his talents. Success depends on self-confidence, on the awareness of one's own talents and of the many possibilities of their adaptation. The awareness of one's own usefulness, the feeling that one can help humanity in various ways, fill the heart with a noble confidence, with an almost religious dignity. But the feeling of independence that results must be born from the ability to be sufficient to oneself and not from a vague liberty due to the benevolent and gratuitous help of adults.

Two "faiths" can raise up the man: faith in God and faith in himself. The two faiths must coexist: the former in the interior life of the man; the latter concerns the social man.

A. REFORMS RELATING TO THE PRESENT FORM OF SOCIETY

The essential reform therefore consists in putting the adolescent in condition to be able to acquire economic independence. It concerns the establishment of an "experimental school of social life."

The "independence" has, in addition, a value more educational than practical. It is more useful to the psychology of the adolescent than to his material life. A boy for whom fortune seems to place material security above the vicissitudes of life must, in spite of the situation, profit greatly from the initiation to economic independence. His personality will be enhanced in that, on the one hand, he will feel able to succeed in life by his own efforts and by his own merits and, on the other, he will be in contact with the supreme reality of life.

The adolescent must, therefore, be placed in a position to earn money by his own efforts. Since we consider that charity is injurious to the indigent so that we strive to give him the possibility of earning what he receives, why do we not apply the same principle to those whose education is in our charge?

The work of which we are speaking must constitute, without any sense of competition, a test of the qualities of the individual, an apprenticeship outside of specialization which permits the talents to reveal themselves.

This concept implies a general principle: to consider work itself to be endowed with greater importance than the kind of work to which one devotes oneself. All work is noble. The only ignoble thing is to live without working. It is essential to understand the value of work in all its forms, be they manual or intellectual. Practical experience will cause the adolescent to understand that the two forms are complementary, and that they are equally essential in a civilized existence.

This concept of education leads to an analogy with what has been in practice since 1837 in certain modern schools of America—secondary schools and universities—and which we owe to Mary Lyon. They are termed "self-help" schools. But the aim of "self-help" is exclusively to give poor students the possibility of earning the price of their studies by means of their own work instead of having them depend on scholarships, which are necessarily limited. The arrangement was put into practice by the schools themselves; that is, it is the school that procures, pays, oversees, and safeguards "self-help." The work is obtained either at the school itself, which is easy in boarding schools, or outside, but always in connection with the organization of the school. This custom is widely developed in the United States of America and the experiment has been crowned with success.

"Self-help" has demonstrated two things:

1. Its high moral relevance. It brings the young people out of the sense of inertia in which one generally finds them when they are passively maintained by their families, and teaches them in a practical manner the value of their time and their own capabilities while making them realize that they are able to participate in social life.

2. The proof that material labor does not retard study but, on the contrary, helps to intensify it: The students obliged to avail themselves of "self-help" are generally those who attain greater scholastic success.

This success supports our assertion that productive work which assures the economic independence of the adolescent or, more exactly, which brings him to the first notion of that independence can advantageously become a general principle for his social education.

In our day the children are delivered to society without any previous preparation. They have to make their experiments without any help, which is a dangerous loss of energy, whereas, if the experience is made with the help of the school, the children are guided by a series of simple and easy experiments. To devote oneself to an agreeable task is restful. All work ought to be presented as having an aim.

We can also consider this plan as a development of the exercises of practical life which have proved themselves with the young children—from even the tiniest in the nursery.

In our "Children's Houses," the three-year-olds learn to dust, to dry, to tidy, to set the table, to serve at table, to wash dishes, et cetera. They learn at the same time to be sufficient to themselves for washing, showering, combing, bathing, dressing, and undressing; for taking their clothes off and arranging them in their locker or in a drawer; for shining their shoes, et cetera.

These exercises form a part of the educational method, without reference to the social situation of the pupils. The children of well-to-do families, used to being surrounded by servants, take part in the "exercises of practical life" when they come to our "Children's Houses." These tasks have an educational rather than a utilitarian aim. And the children react by a veritable explosion of independence as regards all unnecessary assistance which suppresses their activity and prevents their making use of their own powers. Precisely these "independent children" learn to write at four-and-a-half years of age, spontaneously learn to read, and make astounding progress in arithmetic.

The precocious intellectual development of these children well proves that work is not fatiguing. They have revealed the essential need for their development in saying to us: "Help me to do it for myself!"

B. REFORMS RELATING TO THE VITAL NEEDS OF ADOLESCENTS

During the difficult period of adolescence it is desirable to have the child live outside his habitual surroundings, outside the family, in the country, in a peaceful place, in the bosom of nature. There, an existence in the open air, individual treatment, a sound diet ought to be the first conditions for the organization of a center of studies and of work.

This theory is based on the formula that has already been widely tested throughout the world. The creation of secondary schools far from the large cities, in the country or in small cities, goes back a long time. Such institutions have prospered in large number in England for the use of all classes of society, even the most privileged (Eton, Harrow, et cetera), and the same principle may be found in the universities of Oxford, of Cambridge, et cetera. These schools enjoyed such success in Eng-

land and the United States that cities have been built up around
the formerly isolated universities. This is the case of a large part
of the modern universities of America.

Life in the open air, in the sun, a diet rich in vitamins fur-
nished by the nearby fields are the auxiliaries so precious to
the body of the adolescent; while the calm environment, the
silence, the marvels of nature satisfy the mind and are conducive to its functions of reflection and meditation. In addition,
the rhythm of daily life at college can better harmonize with
the demands of study and work, while family life must rather
conform to the demands of the life of the parents.

Our plan, though, is not a simple replica of the universities
in the country or in small cities, because it is not the rural environment itself to which such value is attached, but rather to
rural work and to "work" in general, together with the social
sense conferred by production and earnings.

The observation of nature is not only an enrichment of the
mind from the philosophical and scientific points of view. It is
also at the base of a number of social experiences that engender
the study of civilization and human life.

It is not intended to turn the students into peasants by
means of "rural work." The intensive methods of modern agriculture were not achieved by the manual work of man alone but
equally by his invention. It is thanks to science—a product of
civilization—that man has created a sort of "superconstruction."

Therefore, the work of the soil is at the same time an introduction to nature and to civilization. The work of the soil is the
approach to limitless scientific and historical studies. As for
the harvest that ensues, it constitutes an initiation to the fundamental social mechanism of production and exchange, the economic base on which society rests.

This form of work, then, introduces the children to the heart
of social life by experience and study.

If we have called this organization *Erdkinder,* "The Children of the Soil" or "Rural Children," it is because we are, in fact, dealing with children who are penetrating civilization from its origins—that is to say, from the stage where peoples, settling on parcels of land, commenced a peaceful era of life and of civil progress. The nomads, in the meantime, remained barbarians and warriors.

The children's school or, more exactly, their house in the country or in the small city must provide the opportunity for social experience for them because there their lives are lived on a larger scale and with greater possibility of freedom than with their families.

Various forms of activity should adjoin this establishment. Halfhearted efforts would lead to failure. Work in the hotel, the store, and the farm will complete the whole.

A modern farm requiring a number of scientific and manual labors presents the chance to produce, then to exchange, and also to enter into direct contact with society through the store or sales stand.

By providing a hotel annex, "The Rural Children's Hotel," the school affords itself the opportunity of initiating the children into all that such an enterprise entails.

Such a house, receiving both boys and girls, should be directed by a married couple who, in addition to the material functions, exercise a moral and protective influence on the youths. It would be a family house.

By participating in the administration of the house, the young people acquire experience in all the various branches offered by the hotel enterprise, from the search for comfort to the social and material organization to the surveillance and control of the finances.

Since the small children have proved to us that they were able to keep the house clean and orderly, to serve at table, to wash plates, or to be responsible for the dishes, it will be easy for adolescents to run a hotel. It is a profession for whose preparation special schools have been established.

The hotel with its multiple activities could extend beyond the scope of "residence–hotel" of the children themselves. It could, while remaining simple and rustic, be designed to receive short visits of the families of the pupils, thus permitting them to acquaint themselves with the way of life of their children in school, and contributing to the economic equilibrium of the institution.

The hotel, conceived in a modern design of artistic simplicity and brightened by children free of artificial restraints, ought to furnish a whole range of activities capable of developing the sense of the artistic in one's dwelling.

Finally, another social institution offering very important experiences is the "store." It will be the social center.

A store or sales stand established in the nearby city permits the *Erdkinder* to bring and sell there the products of the fields and gardens together with other products of their labor, and, should the occasion arise, the products of others' labor. They would thus be able to dispose of the products of poor neighbors or tradesmen which do not pass through the normal channels of commerce.

This enterprise should always have its particular characteristics and conserve the tradition of the past when personal talent was expressed in the fabrication of each object.

The store could be considered as the historic resurrection of a medieval shop, which used to be a meeting place and, one could even say, a symbol of sociability. It also offered an artistic aspect. It was consecrated and dedicated by means of a ceremony to some religious idea. It was used for selling and buying in honest simplicity. It constituted a sort of public institution for small commerce where individual exchange of objects took place, bringing with it the exchange of news and sentiments. It was part of the social life.

The ancient custom of mixing business with friendship and the establishment of personal contacts is reminiscent of the past. This custom has every chance of being revived among the joyful, enthusiastic youth avid for variety.

The store, in addition, makes necessary a carefully planned initiation to exchange and commerce. It must teach the art of satisfying a request, of exchanging words and ideas with the man in the street, as well as the strictly accurate keeping of books.

B

Study and Work Plans

Study and Work Plans

IT IS impossible to establish a priori a detailed program of studies and work. Only a general plan can be outlined here. The program, supported by experience, should establish itself very naturally.

The studies are not necessarily tied from the beginning to the present programs of secondary schools. They ought much less to borrow the "methods" in existence. They must, though, enlarge and not reduce the field of knowledge. Reform is principally required in the *manner* of distributing knowledge and in the "methods" of teaching.

Our plan aims above all at making possible the development of the personality in the present social conditions. Such an education, therefore, cannot rightfully be restricted to a specialization of instruction capable of assuring "a good position" for the future. The necessity of specialization being absolutely disastrous, such specialization must not be considered as a "goal" to which both the values of the individual and his feeling of responsibility to society are to be sacrificed, but rather as a "practical means" of entering into society.

Two essential principles:

1. It is not necessary to resort to "vacations" to rest. They are a loss of time and break the continuity of life. Rest comes

from a *change of occupations*. Vacations can therefore be obtained by varying occupations, by diversifying interests.

2. Study answers a "need of the intelligence." If it is organized to correspond to the psychic nature of the individual, not only does it not cause "mental fatigue" but it answers a need, thereby regenerating and strengthening the development of the mind.

These two principles have already been demonstrated in our "Children's Houses." Studies and work that do not cause any fatigue greatly increase the will of the young children so that they, indefatigable, continue to work after going home.

During our first experience, the children arrived at eight in the morning and left at six in the evening. And yet they carried materials away from the school in order to be able to continue their work at home. At least as much ardor may be found among adolescents.

But, to obtain such a result, it is necessary "to second" nature by answering the needs peculiar to each age. Experience must be the guide.

A. ATTENTION TO SOCIAL MORALITY

By "attention to social morality" we understand the relations that need to be established between the children, the teachers, and those around them. The teachers must treat the young personalities with the greatest respect. Great riches are hidden in the soul of each child. Our hope of future progress resides in the minds of the young boys and girls. What is more, it is they who are the judges of the present.

It is in the *mystery of the adolescent* that the innermost calling of man is found.

If social progress is realized during the course of generations, the development of these children once they have become adults in their turn will be superior to that of their present teachers.

One can find something in each adolescent that symbolizes Jesus feeling himself tied to a Father who makes him forget his earthly parents, and astonishing the sages and elders with his knowledge. Let us never forget that "Jesus followed his parents in obedience and worked submissively in preparing for his future mission."

Respect for young people is essential. One must never treat adolescents as children. They have passed that stage. It is of greater value to treat them as if their worth were superior to their real worth than to minimize their merits and risk injury to their sense of personal dignity.

The young must be left with sufficient liberty to act according to individual initiative. Let us, then, prepare the means while leaving them the liberty to create. But, in order that individual action be simultaneously free and fruitful, it must be confined within certain limits and obey certain rules which constitute the necessary direction. The limits and rules must be observed by the entire institution. One must not give the adolescents the impression that they are not conscientious, that they are unable to discipline themselves.

The rules, like the materials for the youngest children, must be "necessary and sufficient" to maintain order and assure progress. The organization must be conceived in such a way that the adolescents do not feel in any way out of place as a consequence, and so that they may adapt in any surroundings.

The adaptation will then manifest itself by "collaboration," source of the social harmony which accelerates individual progress.

The surroundings ought to make "free choice" easy. But it is necessary to guide the child so that he does not waste his time and energy in aimless activity.

From the set of these preparations will arise not only discipline but also the proof that discipline is an aspect of individual liberty, an essential factor of success in life.

It is indispensable to hold to an order in which the occupations follow one another during the day and to choose well the moment of change. That is to say, it is necessary to take advantage of opportunities that offer themselves and that concur with a logical order.

Along with this consideration of the active occupations, one must also do justice to the need for calm and solitude, two essential requirements of the adolescent.

B. PHYSICAL EDUCATION

Given the physical conditions of adolescence, the treatment of the body requires very special attention. This is a critical period during which all the endocrine glands are active, and, through this, the whole organism. The body grows rapidly, but not at a uniform pace, so that a functional imbalance results. In the first adolescent period, the legs increase in length much faster than the trunk and, as a consequence, than the thorax. This results in an insufficiency of the heart which causes palpitations and the waning of the resistance of the lungs. Muscular strength does not increase in proportion to the height and leg length either. Sometimes one would divide adolescence into three periods:

1. The development of the legs.
2. The development of the trunk and especially the chest.
3. The development of muscular strength.

And since the changes are produced at close intervals during approximately two years, it is good to observe closely the growth of the adolescent and to take anthropometric measurements as well as to make periodic checks of heart and lungs, even when an adolescent seems to be in perfect health.

Particular attention must be paid to diet. It must be both abundant and nutritious but without meat during this period. In rural locations where vegetables, fruits, eggs, and milk products conserve all their value, foods such as raw vegetables and especially fruit accompanied by milk, milk substitutes, and eggs must abound in the menus. Freshly gathered vegetables and fruits that have been allowed to mature on the plants are veritable treasures. Wilted vegetables and artificially grown fruits, such as one most often buys in the city, have insufficient nutritive value.

The ordinary poisons, alcohol and tobacco, must be banished. They may be replaced by candy because sugar has nutritive value of primary necessity for the adolescent to almost the same degree as for the infant.

Life in the open air and sunshine, bathing, and swimming ought to occur as frequently as possible—almost as in the sanatorium. Flat terrain, where long walks are easy, on the seashore or in the woods, is preferable to a high mountain where hikes may strain the heart at this stage of development when the chest is insufficiently developed.

C. PROGRAM AND METHODS

The general program of studies may be divided into three parts. It is necessary:

1. To open the way to the possibilities of the adolescent for personal expression, that is, to facilitate, by exercises and exterior means, the development of the interior personality.

2. To supply that which we consider to be the creative elements necessary for the physical being of man in general.

3. To put the adolescent into relation with present civilization by bringing him general culture and by experience.

1. *To open the way to the possibilities of personal expression.*

The exercises to this end are the artistic exercises left to free choice, as much for the type of exercise as for the moment of its taking place. Certain children choose individual, others group work. The exercises are related to the arts, to language, and to the imagination. They include music, dramatic art and diction, and art tasks.

a. *Music:* The execution of excerpts by which the children learn to identify the composers and their periods, as is currently done in literary studies. Choirs. The study of instruments, either solo or orchestral.

b. *Language:* Diction, elocution, dramatic or poetic representations. To cultivate the art of speaking logically, to expose one's ideas, to reason, and to discuss. Reading aloud so as to hold the attention of the public, free conferences on personal ideas.

c. *Art tasks:* Drawing, solid representations, modeling with plastic substances, et cetera, with various aims such as ornamental drawings, reproductions from nature, creations from the imagination, et cetera. At this point we are not considering these tasks as the true study of art. They are only intended to facilitate the expression of personal artistic feeling, to relate to manual work, and to assist in the acquisition of modern techniques.

2. *To supply that which we consider to be the creative elements necessary for the physical being of man in general.*

The child needs to be put to the test. His instinct causes him to see the beauty in everything, encourages him to admire everything. We must favor this tendency. His personality needs to be observed and helped, on condition that the help is limited to the need. If we wish to give him religious education adapted to his age, it must be effected through contacts. God loves His creation, watches it constantly, never abandons it. If we wish to give a religious concept of nature we must always speak of the individual, of the animal in the singular—and, to be very clear, very distinct, one could say dissected, ground, analyzed: the child, the father, the mother, the persons, the animals. We are facilitating the construction of the personality during this period. We are also trying to dispel confusion by materializing everything, even to render the abstract possible of being touched and manipulated by the hands.

"Creative" culture, intended to develop the very bases of the personality, divides into three branches: moral education, mathematics, and languages.

a. *Moral education* constructs the base of the spiritual equilibrium on which repose all the rest, and which may be compared to the physical equilibrium without which it is impossible to maintain oneself erect, let alone put oneself to purposeful movement.

b. *Mathematics:* Human intelligence today is no longer a natural intelligence but a mathematical intelligence. Without a mathematical education it is impossible to understand the progress of our time or to participate in it. In our time, a mind without mathematical culture is comparable to that of a man ignorant of the alphabet at the time when literary culture again came to the forefront. In its natural state the human mind is already mathematical: it tends toward exactness, measure, and comparison. It is capable, within limits, of penetrating the numerous "effects" that nature offers mankind while it hides the world of "causes."

It is necessary then, because of the vital importance of mathematics, that the school employ "special methods" in its teaching of the subject and that it render the individual concepts clear and understandable by the help of concrete examples.

c. *Languages:* The development of language is a part of the personality itself. Words are, in effect, the natural means to express an idea and consequently to establish understanding between men. If formerly a single language sufficed, today it is essential to teach different languages. Latin, whose importance was great at the time when literary culture was the principal culture, is not so essential in our day. The teaching of it ought, in any case, never to be "imposed" since it is practically useless except for classical studies with a professional view. Latin, though, has sufficient historic importance that its acquisition ought always to be possible for those who desire it. It ought, then, to be available as an optional subject. The teachers of Latin thus have the opportunity of influencing the student by making attractive the language that reflects the origins of our civilization.

3. *To put the adolescent into relation with present civilization by bringing him general culture and by experience.*

a. *The study of the earth and living nature:* Geology (with documentation on prehistoric ages), biology, cosmography, botany, zoology, physiology, astronomy, and comparative anatomy.

b. *Studies relating to human progress and to the building of civilization by means of the physical, chemical, and other sciences.* Even though exact, these studies must always include practical experiments to give the children the opportunity to observe and to experiment for themselves. Thanks to such a base, the students will be able to assimilate the most difficult subjects, impossible of demonstration in a school. The practical concepts, while illustrating theory, make it more attractive and engage the students to go ever onward.

The school will have to own its "museum of machines": manageable machines, permitting the children to disassemble and reassemble them, to use them on occasion, to repair them.

The inclined plane, gears, the pulley, the wheel, and all items that help in obtaining greater force with less effort; lenses and prisms for the concentration and direction of light can constitute the equipment for the study of the essential laws of physics with their formulas and mathematical calculations. The same for statics: simple equipment may be conceived which will help to understand the laws governing the equilibrium of buildings and bridges.

The *Erdkind* must be accustomed to using machines: typewriters, knitting machines, weaving machines, calculators, printing presses; to photograph, to develop; projectors, microscopes, phonographs and radios, electric machines. He ought to know the Morse code for telegraphy and to manage the machines of modern life—not only the bicycle "to go faster," but also the little machines of common usage: vegetable peelers, food grinders, vacuum cleaners, washing and ironing machines, et cetera. This is a multiform organ of the life of modern man.

Here the thought imposes itself: Civilization has given man, by means of the machine, power much greater than his own. But for the work of civilization to develop, man must also develop. The malady from which our age suffers comes from the imbalance created by the difference in rhythm at which man and machine have evolved; the machine has advanced at an accelerated pace and man has remained behind. Man is dependent on the machine while it is he who must dominate it. Progress must not mean the triumph of materialism. It ought, on the contrary, "to elevate" man. Placing one's ideals at ever higher levels is exalting. We must teach the adolescents what our task on earth is. But the power man has gained from the use of the machine ought also to create new duties, an always higher morality.

Man by means of supranatural powers may perceive through glass infinitely small or distant things. He can make mathematical calculations that would have been completely inaccessible and even inconceivable to natural man. He can today listen to voices that have come a considerable distance. He can measure the waves that render communication possible. He travels at an always faster speed; he flies in the air and maintains himself on the surface of the sea. The machine therefore confers on him an immense power, a power almost as fantastic as that of the heroes of fairy tales. The progress of the social surroundings is related to it. But if education does not help him to participate in such a world, he remains "outside society." Man with this "supernature" is the king of the earth, of visible and invisible things. He penetrates the secrets of life by giving birth to the flora and fauna that constitute such a supernature, causing products of the earth to progress by chemistry, transforming bodies as though by the help of a magic wand. This is the proof of the grandeur of collective humanity, to which each man can contribute. But it is also because of this that the man who has such power becomes dangerous. New individual and social morals are necessary in the new world—morals that give new directives on good and evil, on the heavy responsibilities individuals are assuming in regard to the whole of humanity, from the moment their power rises above that of their nature proper. The machine ought not to *replace the slave* in the new civilization.

c. *The history of humanity,* which ought to be as complete as possible. We must give the complete view in which it is good to choose particular periods for individual studies. A specialized library having geographic atlases; a history museum, i.e., pictures and reproductions of historic and prehistoric documents —this, among the rest of what is in the library, constitute precious material.

The most important part of history for adolescents is that which treats explorations and inventions. It is good to illustrate history with images of the social life before and after the discovery in question with a view to comparing the life of man in the course of the different stages of civilization.

Another facet of history particularly suited to the following period is that which treats human development in relation to geographic events: contacts and cross-breedings among the different peoples, the assimilation of different races and cultures, the wars and the conquests of empires—all accompanied by an examination of feelings and customs, of the influence of religion and patriotic sentiment, and the behavior of man.

Special subjects: In addition to these considerations of a general nature, it is interesting to dedicate oneself to a detailed study of an era, an event, or the life of a personage arousing particular interest in the students. It is an opportunity to collect, consult, and compare the documents, articles, and pictures until total comprehension of the subject is attained.

It is necessary to look at the present state of the country, its constitution, its laws, its particular characteristics, and its moral character, all of which ought to be copiously illustrated with references. Visits to places having a particular historic interest ought also to be undertaken.

The Methods

The best methods are those that arouse maximum interest in the student, that give him the opportunity to work alone, to experiment by himself, and that permit him to alternate his studies with the practical life.

A schema, written in large letters, posted in an obvious position, clearly indicating the degree of study demanded by the laws governing secondary education, constitutes an excellent stimulant and gives the directives but not the obligations. Furthermore, it is necessary to let those who wish to work have the opportunity to attain—or even to surpass—the level required by official regulation.

The school of the *Erdkind* covers all the period of puberty, up to eighteen years. During the last two years it is necessary to assist the pupils in preparing for the university or to pass the examinations required to obtain diplomas.

Practical Considerations

A plan of study from which we presently find ourselves at such a great distance can only be realized little by little. It is of course understood that we are speaking of a school that is open to all children who have passed through the elementary school, and not only to those coming from specialized schools; from schools for normal children but where slow or retarded children, or those simply suffering from some psychic fault such as a mental block or shyness, may be sure to find efficient help to obtain effective betterment.

A large space with trees, near the sea, and at the same time near a city, are prerequisites of the best site for the establishment of such a school. The teachers should have the possibility of living in the school itself, taking upon themselves a part of the chores and participating in the life of the house. A severe discipline ought to exist for the personnel attached to the institution as well as for the students, in order to assure an ordered inner life and the unity of aims. The adolescents will necessarily adapt to orderly surroundings.

The young teachers—men and women—will also come from outside to teach. They must, of course, be qualified to teach in a secondary school. But that does not mean that they will be free to teach by their own methods. On the contrary, they must adopt the methods of the institution in order for their collaboration to be effective. The teachers must be young, of open minds, ready to take an active part in the life of the school and to contribute personally. On the other hand, they ought not to be present in too great number: the minimum capable of teaching the material according to the requirements arising from the methods of the school.

In addition to teachers for the usual subjects, it is necessary to add technicians, such as a teacher of agriculture and horticulture, another who contributes business knowledge such as the running of a store or hotel, and a teacher of artistic work. All the members of the staff ought to be specially qualified for the practical work their subject involves: cooking, sewing, repairing, and bookkeeping. It is equally desirable to obtain the services of an intelligent workman who knows how to do the many jobs required in a household.

Just as our young children in the elementary schools have learned to fold their things, to sew, to put things in order, so these must learn to repair broken objects, to put a machine into service or to fix a piece of furniture, to replace a square of linoleum, to repair a lock, et cetera. They must be able to blaze a trail, to improvise a sounding device, to saw wood, and perform other little tasks.

One may ask how they will earn money. Profit, which cannot be immediate, cannot be obtained except by the help of adults. The adults in fact must first earn the money and thus give the example of the way to work, and then let the children participate little by little in the material and economic organization and in the execution of tasks. For example, an already existing modern farm or a garden where flowers are cultured can utilize the help of children, a few at a time. An arrangement between the school and the neighboring establishments would suffice.

In this way the store could be created by a committee of adults, by the families of the pupils. An adult must assume responsibility. But the children, cooperating by turns, would contribute their note of youthful gaiety at the same time they provide their energy and ingenuity to the work.

The establishment must grow by collaboration between the parents, the technicians, and the children themselves.

It would be good to follow this month's preparation period by a sort of examination, which would not relate to studies but to problems of conscience. It is, in effect, at this moment that the child makes a sort of debut into life. It is at this time that we must prepare him to fight against the evil forces which he will find himself. He must resist temptations. Also, we cannot let him present himself before the "prince of this earth" without any preparation: a resumé of what he has done up to now and an examination of conscience constitute a sort of admission to the entrance into life.

C

The Function of the University

The Function of the University

SCHOOLS EXIST for children and adolescents. Only one school is intended for adults: the university.

After the age of eighteen years, the "preparation of the organism" is complete, and the laws recognize the physical maturity of the individual in permitting him to marry. At twenty-one years of age, man is considered to be free. He is no longer a minor.

In general, a person enters the university after the age of eighteen and continues to attend until twenty-one, and even two or three years after that. The university, therefore, is a school for adults.

This consideration, being of a merely physical order, is the only one that places the university in a position different from that of the other schools.

And yet it is constituted in a manner that resembles the other schools. It is nothing other than a direct continuation of them. The students continue to follow lessons, to listen to teachers, to pass examinations on which their career depends. The only difference is that the university students are not made to repeat the lessons or to do homework—which is to say that, among people used to continuously controlled hard work, they work less. In addition, they have longer vacations. Furthermore, just as previously, they are dependent on their families who watch over the success of their studies from a financial point of view: a success they measure by examination results and grades.

At the university, men live as children even though they are men. This is where they ought to become conscious of their responsibilities, of their role, which is to create a family. Instead, they generally show a lack of conscientiousness. They form erroneous ideas of life. One cannot hope that such men will contribute to the betterment of society.

In the Middle Ages, the life of students had the stamp of grandeur and dignity. There existed centers of study such as the celebrated University of Bologna, which received young men from all the countries of Europe. Each of these students was aware of his intellectual responsibility toward his country of origin, which was honored to count its citizens among those attending the university. The University of Bologna sumptuously displayed on the walls of its large amphitheater the arms, in gold and in enamel, of the cities and states represented. The students participated in philosophic and political discussions which caused them to become aware of their true value and of the moral responsibilities belonging to them. The solemnity of the formalities, the ermine robes of the professors, were constant reminders of the special dignity of such centers. In the old universities, there were no examinations except that for the doctorate. The students, having an overpowering interest in the acquisition of higher learning, occupied themselves with their studies. Their time was measured. It was precious. The university celebrations, inspired by a regard for the artistic, constituted events of public life. The universities were "centers of culture" from which radiated civilization with universal aims. And the students —that is, those who were studious—became its propagators.

But today civilization and culture are transmitted by other means, which are both more extensive and easier. Culture is propagated by the press and by rapid communications, which establish a sort of universal leveling.

Moreover, the universities have become, little by little, simple professional schools where only the degree of schooling is superior to that of the other schools. But they have lost their sense of dignity and grandeur which made them a central instrument for the progress of civilization.

The students, having as their aim only to obtain some obscure post for themselves, can no longer have the sense of mission that formerly created the "spirit of the university." The desire to work as little as possible, to pass the exams at all costs, and to obtain the diploma that will serve each person's individual interests has become the essential motive common to the students. Thus academic institutions have become decadent as the progress of culture has transformed man's existence. True centers of progress have been established in the laboratories of the scientific researchers. They are closed places, foreign to the common culture.

The general decadence of the schools noted in our day does not come from a lessening of the instruction given to the students but from a lack of concordance between the organization of the schools and today's needs. The schools have remained below the level of civilization attained on the outside. The material bases of civilization have changed to the point where they announce the beginning of a new civilization. In this critical period of human history, the very life of men needs to adapt afresh. And it is here that the problem of education is to be found.

Education does not consist in discovering new methods useful in the arid transfusion of knowledge. It must have the purpose of helping man. We must therefore consider human life and its values. If the "formation of man" becomes the basis of education, it will be necessary to establish coordination between all phases from childhood to maturity, from the nursery to the university. Because a man—even though he passes through interdependent phases—is nonetheless a single entity. The preceding level prepares for what follows by laying the foundations, by stimulating energies. The lack of coordination between the successive levels of School are already an obstacle in the schools, even such as exist today. Universities have their own plan of study, but they find the students insufficiently prepared to follow it; it is the same in the secondary school with reference to the elementary school. And everybody feels the burdensome obstacle that is the lack of preparation of the personality.

Furthermore, if education is intended to develop the man as well as the culture, a rigorous coordination becomes essential and indispensable to all the periods of life.

During the course of our experiments with the elementary-school children, we have noted that it is exactly between the ages of six and twelve years that the bases of all the sciences ought to be constructed. There exists at that time a psychologically sensitive period that could be called "the sensitive period for culture," during which the abstract structure of the human mind is organized. It is at that time that all must be sown. One can compare this period of the human mind to a field where seeds of grain are thrown which then await their respective season to germinate.

The aim of education is to study all possible means to "sow the seed" at the suitable age. The "seeding" ought to interest not only the elementary schools but also the university, in the same way that the planting of flax ought also to interest the canvas-maker, since it becomes useless to have good instruments to work the raw material if the latter is wanting.

Psychological life proceeds in the same manner. At certain ages an inner activity forms the roots of the first intellectual development, thus arousing enthusiastic reactions and awakening the capacities that, without such activity, would remain half-dormant. There follows the whole age of youth which develops these centers of interest. But if the seeds of knowledge have not been sown at the right season, only an inertia remains, which causes the child to balk at effort, and all study is sterile. One could say that it is when one has committed this sin against the laws of life that work becomes an arid effort, a sort of condemnation similar to that described in the Bible regarding Adam. Evidently it is not work, but work outside the laws, that is condemned by the divine curse. It is thus that the student follows a dry course in a forced manner and without animation. A supreme encouragement would be necessary, a ray of light to call out the hearts that are withdrawn into themselves by inertia and error, to revive the languishing life. But it is not a dry school that can do this, one that underestimates the personality of the student and continues to aggravate his discouragement and inertia.

Therefore, even for the acquisition of knowledge the various phases of school have a common interest. Or rather, the higher schools have, with regard to the elementary schools, a concern with control. For it is in the latter that human energies are prepared.

The university professors, as much those of the sciences as of letters, will have before them ardent apostles, intelligent critics, and veritable collaborators in their students if these have developed normally. If not, they will have before them resistant, indifferent, and inert minds, disrespectful youths whom they will have to keep on a leash as so many young goats.

But collaboration is still more necessary when treating of the human personality in its totality, because man is thirsty not only for culture. Culture brings with it something receptive, while life is active and expansive and seeks creativity outside itself. Which is to say that to study is not to live; but to live is precisely what is most necessary in order to be able to study.

In the same way we have noted that study, even in the

broadest terms and even when assimilated, does not satisfy the human personality. Other needs remain whose lack of satisfaction leads to inner conflicts having an influence on the mental state, whose clarity is disturbed by them. Joy, the sensibility of one's just value, feeling appreciated and loved by others, feeling useful and able to produce—these are factors of immense interest to the human spirit. The new university will have to draw its new dignity from these factors and not only from culture. The moral and philosophical considerations of life and the aims of man used to be the basis of the university. Culture used to be the splendid *means* to raise humanity to a higher level. Today it is not by philosophy, not by discussion of metaphysical concepts, that the morals of mankind can be raised. It is by activity, by experience, and by action.

It is interesting to note how much all the practical actions interest the child during the period preceding adolescence. Manual work, having a practical aim, aids in the acquisition of an inner discipline. When a skill is perfected in a freely chosen field, and it creates the will to succeed and to overcome obstacles, something more than a simple accomplishment has occurred; a feeling of one's own worth has developed. From the tenderest age, man gains most satisfaction from a feeling of independence. The feeling of being sufficient to oneself comes unexpectedly as a revelation. There can be no doubt that this is a fundamental element of social life.

It is very evident that the need to help others or to seek their collaboration cannot manifest itself when one is entirely dependent on them and when one is convinced of one's own inadequacy. Finally, vital energies consist in the sense of one's true value and in the knowledge of the possibility of participating in a social organization. They are not acquired only by memorizing lessons or by resolving problems having nothing to do with practical life.

Life must become the focal point, and education the means. Nothing shows the need for education better than to experiment to see how necessary it is to live intelligently and consciously. To understand the essential help it brings, to feel its need in order to succeed, and, as a consequence, to consider it the source of spiritual joy are what drive one to study more and more.

The relationship that exists between life and education is proof that children are open to the acquisition of considerably more than what today's school pretends to teach through its programs. The first interest must be aroused during childhood in order to provide the seeding of all the sciences.

Man grows as a whole, and if the development of an essential part of him fails to occur, complexes arise which can cause disturbances even to the brain.

One who becomes conscious of his just value becomes naturally predisposed to association. We have seen how association among children occurs spontaneously, all by itself, for purposes of thinking and of understanding. It seems that true comprehension goes hand in hand with discussion, with criticism, and with the approval of others. It is necessary that the pleasure of knowing be immediately communicated to someone else. Enthusiasm is developed by such communication.

Study and thought call for association just as does manual work. Whoever lends himself to a task too difficult for him needs to associate with other individuals. The help of others is also necessary in order to understand. Spontaneous collaboration is a truly revealing manifestation.

Association brings new strength with it. It stimulates new energies. Human nature needs society as much for thought as for action.

All the points noted put the finger on the impossibility of enclosing education within the limits of a room where the individual at work is inert, perpetually dependent on the teacher, separated from the rest of mankind. This is true even for small children.

The first reform of education must be to offer children vaster horizons, more varied activities, and the possibilities of working in association.

A germination period for the construction of society occurs precisely during adolescence. Society builds itself by means of various kinds of activities, not only by purely intellectual ones. And above all, it requires that the individual who is developing his social experiences acquire a growing feeling of his own consciousness.

An inert child who has never worked with his hands, who has never sensed that "to live" means to live socially, and that, to think and to create, it is necessary first to achieve harmony of the soul—that child will be a selfish, pessimistic, and melancholy adolescent who will seek the compensations of a lost paradise in the superficial values of vanity. It is thus that he will present himself at the doors of the university. To ask for what? To ask for a profession that will assure his material life in a society which is strange and indifferent to him, and to participate in a civilization of which he is ignorant.

It is not possible to contemplate the man only after he has become a man. We must study him earlier. If we wish to find a man one day, we must first have sought the child. To separate the different phases of his life is absurd. The man is the result of the child. The causes of the good and evil one finds in the adult could have been discovered during the course of the brief growth period of the child.

The distinction we attach to the interests of the child as opposed to those of the adult, in education as in social questions, makes me think of a battle between two countries that during the Middle Ages claimed to own religious relics. One possessed the three skulls of the Wise Men as children, and the other the three skulls of the Wise Men as adults.

This sort of psychic barrier that neatly separates the two interests, this fatal criterion, is the basis of serious errors and constitutes a danger to civilized humanity. Why, before all the perils that threaten the future of all peoples, does one not consider the supreme defense—that which consists in caring for, fortifying, and preparing humanity by all means possible—while it is still in the formative stage?

Today, in our miraculous society, what is lacking is the spiritual force in mankind; moral force is missing, but above all we lack the sense that human life should triumph.

The man who arrives at the university has left behind him both childhood and adolescence. He is a man already formed. To a very large extent his social destiny and the success of his studies depend on the way in which he has been formed.

The "goal of man" is what is important to us. Such a goal cannot be reduced to the mere storage of knowledge necessary for practicing a profession. The students are adults who will exercise an influence on the civilization of their time. Educators, and as a consequence the leaders of the new humanity, come from the university. The leaders of the masses and the defenders of civilization also come from the university. When they have passed their examinations, and thus find themselves before the portals of the world, they will still need serious moral preparation. Once they are men, they will not remain in school simply in order to know a little more than the others. Culture, it is true, represents a large part of their preparation. But these men, thanks to this means, are open to discover everything. The social ambiance is infiltrated by culture. It is therefore important to intensify it and to make it penetrate man's consciousness. It is a defense mechanism for humanity and for civilization.

Religion, which is available to all, takes on a more penetrating intensity in missionaries and priests, which makes them work for the good of mankind. In the same way culture, which exists everywhere and which has reached a plateau among civilized peoples, takes on a deeper form among a few elect who make themselves the apostles of it in order to sustain it.

Preparation ought therefore to be more extensive and more

active at the university. If the process of the children's education cannot be carried out in the confines of four walls, that of adults is still less capable of being carried out satisfactorily there. An adolescent must feel that he is independent. The man must already have achieved his independence. Social experiences must continue.

A man who has never worked, who has never tried to earn his living, who has never approached the different age levels and the different social classes, will have great difficulty being worthy of a position of leadership.

The "value of the personality" must be actively cultivated by concrete experiences. The consciousness of modern man will not be formed by philosophizing, nor by meditating.

The very function of the university is teaching to study. The diploma is nothing more than the proof that one knows how to study, that one knows how to acquire culture by oneself, that one has been shown the way to do scientific research. This is the proof that instruction is not the essential task of the university. If one has learned to learn, it is for the purpose of learning. The man with a diploma, then, is one who knows how to navigate better on the ocean of culture. He has received an orientation. He is a worker who has a compass that puts him in communication with the stars that light his way. That is what a man with a diploma is.

If the diploma is nothing else than a certificate of ability to learn, why must university studies take from three to six years? A man who studies at the university knows that it is necessary to study all his life or study will lose all its value. Why then must he endure these several years of harassment to acquire a body of knowledge which will never be complete? Another aid to the education of these young men must exist—one that would permit them to become a part of their society and to adapt to contemporary needs.

It would be a great advantage for a true student to achieve

his financial independence during his university studies. Many young people are already teachers in private schools, journalists, artists, assistants, at work in business, et cetera. Many are already employed in laboratories or in diplomatic tasks. Such workers have greater chances of working for the love of study, with a view to human progress, and not just to achieve immediate aims. If it takes them a few more years to complete their studies, it matters little, since their studies are never to finish!

It is the same for those desiring to become university professors. They study but do not go to school. However, they do make a modest living. They do this for the precise purpose of being able to study and to attain always higher goals. It is not necessary for a man who studies to be preoccupied by an examination like a child who fears a scolding from his father. It is not necessary to look for tricks to obtain good marks. A man ought, above all, to know how to find his own independence and his own social equilibrium. And all facilities ought to be provided to create some form of work that may permit the students to get a start toward economic independence, so that they may be entirely free to study and able to find their true position according to their just value.

One could compare the life of a man to the three stages of the life of Christ: First the child, miraculous and sublime— the age of "creative sensitivity," of mental construction so intense in the activities needed to deposit the seeds of culture.

The age of adolescence follows: the age of interior revelations, of social sensitivities. It is at this age that Christ, an adolescent, reasoned with the scholars outside of his immediate family. He did not speak as a scholar but as a master of overpowering brilliance. And then he dedicated himself to manual tasks and followed a trade.

Finally there is the man who prepares himself for his mission on earth. What is it that he does to prepare himself? He confronts the devil and wins. That is the preparation. A man has the strength to recognize and confront the dangers and the temptations of the world in order to fight against them and overcome them. In the literal sense, the temptations to overcome are those of the Gospel: the temptation of possession and the temptation of power. Something exists within man that is above temptation. He can understand the only means to create a purified, powerful, and rich world: to know how to overcome, individually, the temptation to possession and power.

That is the way to his kingdom. But to find it by education, one must look to the child and contemplate him from a different point of view.

Index